Sew Magical for Baby

Vice President and Chief Operations Officer: Tom Siebenmorgen
Vice President, Sales and Marketing: Pam Stebbins
Vice President, Operations: Jim Dittrich
Editor in Chief: Susan White Sullivan
Director of Designer Relations: Debra Nettles
Senior Art Director: Rhonda Shelby
Senior Prepress Director: Mark Hawkins

Produced for Leisure Arts, Inc. by Penn Publishing Ltd.
www.penn.co.il
Editor: Shoshana Brickman
Design and layout: Ariane Rybski
Photography by: Danya Weiner
Illustrations by: Laura Lee Burch
Technical editor: Rita Greenfeld

PRINTED IN CHINA

ISBN-13: 978-1-57486-328-4
ISBN-10: 1-57486-328-2
Library of Congress Control Number: 2009940597

Cover photography by Danya Weiner

Sew Magical for Baby

by

LAURA LEE BURCH

A LEISURE ARTS PUBLICATION

Contents

Introduction

In many parts of the world, sewing has always been, and continues to be, part of a woman's basic training. Mothers and grandmothers teach their daughters basic sewing techniques so that they can sew on buttons, hem dresses and pants, mend ripped clothing, and make costumes. In my family, we didn't always go out to buy new items, but often made them ourselves, especially for special occasions.

Growing up, I watched my mother and grandmother make clothing, bedding, toys, and gifts for the family. Handcrafted items were handed down from one child to another, and from one generation to the next. We knew these items were special, because someone we loved had made them.

In recent years, people have begun to realize the importance and utility of handmade items again. Like my mother and grandmother before me, I love making special things for my daughters. The dolls, toys, and costumes I make for my children are accompanied by stories and memories; they are unique, durable, and made with high quality materials. My girls have been watching me make things since they were young; now I see them designing and making their own items. Thus, the circle of creativity continues.

A Bit About Me

The inspiration for this book originated in my children's boutique, Burch and Daughters (www.lauraleeburch.com), which is a magical world of my handmade toys, costumes, dolls, and other creations inspired by my childhood and my daughters. One of my goals is to instill a sense of pride in my daughters, and to provide them with a connection to their cultural heritage.

When people wander into my boutique, they are astounded to see so many items that bring back memories of their own childhood. They often say they've never seen so many magical items...and all of them are handmade! With this book, I hope readers learn to make their own magical items, creating wonderful memories for their children and loved ones.

Acknowledgements

I would like to thank my family for being patient with me as I worked during "family time," and my three daughters for inspiring me. I'd like to thank the very talented Renana Una, and Natalia Sohovolski, for helping to make my ideas and designs come to life. I would never have come to this point in my artistic life if my Grandma Burch hadn't been such an extremely creative seamstress, nor if my Grandfather Perkinson hadn't been so proud of me even when I won second place in the art shows I entered as a child. Thank you to Anat Avrahami-Harnik, to whom I owe my positive creative attitude, even when I'm not positive. Thank you to Limore Aloni, for letting her adorable daughter Yaeli model for the book. Thank you to Rachel and Elan Penn who liked my work enough to help me write a book about it and mostly, thank you to my best friend and husband Doron Levitas who has helped me to be artful since we first met.

Laura Lee Burch

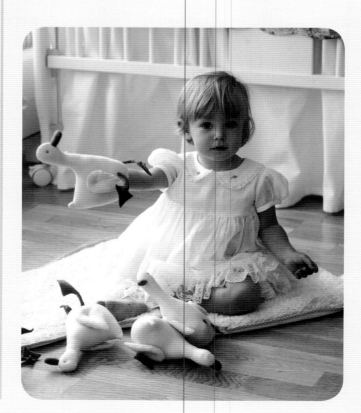

Before You Start

Embroidery Stitches

Satin Stitch

This smooth, decorative stitch is good for making noses on stuffed animals (Figure A).

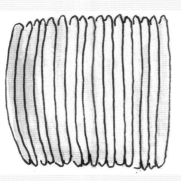

Figure A

Running stitch

This fast, in/out stitch makes straight lines (Figure B).

Figure B

Blanket stitch

This decorative stitch is sewn along fabric edges to prevent fraying.

STEP 1

Knot thread and bring needle up through fabric.

STEP 2

Make a small stitch, perpendicular to the edge of your project (Figure C).

STEP 3

Start sewing about ¼" (0.6 cm) away from the edge, and stitch down.

STEP 4

Make sure loose part of thread is under the needle as you pull the stitch through the fabric (Figures D and E).

Figure C

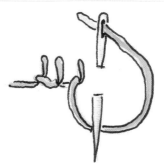

Figure D

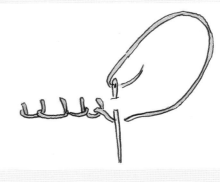

Figure E

French knot

Excellent for making eyes on dolls and stuffed animals or for adding a decorative touch to embroidered pieces.

STEP 1

Knot thread and bring needle up through fabric.

STEP 2

Pull needle halfway through fabric at spot where you want French knot.

STEP 3

Wrap thread around the needle 6 or 7 times.

STEP 4

Pull needle rest of the way through fabric and wrapped embroidery thread, keeping thread together with your fingers.

STEP 5

Once needle has been pulled through fabric and thread has been wrapped around needle, keep pulling thread with needle until wrapped thread knots to form a small ball (Figure F).

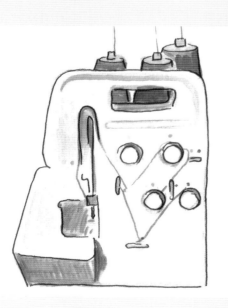

Figure F

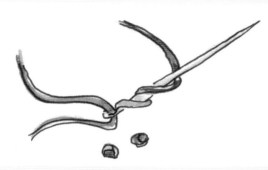

Backstitch

This simple stitch goes from right to left and can be used to make the lines of a smile on a stuffed animal's face.

STEP 1

Knot thread and bring needle up through fabric. Make a stitch.

STEP 2

From backside of fabric, poke needle through fabric, ahead of first stitch, at approximately the same length as the first stitch.

STEP 3

Complete second stitch by placing needle at beginning of first stitch.

STEP 4

Continue in this manner to make a line (Figure G).

Figure G

Non-Embroidery Stitches

Slipstitch

This is used to close openings in stuffed animals and other projects.

STEP 1

Knot thread and bring needle up through fabric. Make a small stitch through folded edge of fabric.

STEP 2

Make another stitch through folded edge of fabric, on other side. Continue sewing from one side to the other (Figure H). Stitches should be very hard to see.

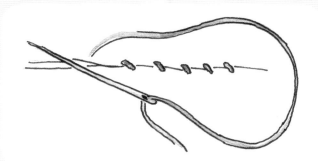

Figure H

Experience Level

The row of bunnies at the top of each project indicates the level of difficulty. One orange bunny indicates that the project is easy and just right for beginners; five orange bunnies indicates that the project is challenging, and more suitable for experienced sewers.

Tips

- Always work with unwrinkled fabric.
- All seam allowances should be the width of the presser foot, unless otherwise instructed.
- After sewing curved seams, make several small snips on wrong side edge of fabric, along seam at curves. Take care not to cut stitches.
- Always trim corners before turning projects right side out.
- I prefer embroidering eyes onto animal faces (rather than using doll eyes, beads, or buttons) so that their eyes can't fall off and pose a hazard to curious babies.
- If possible, leave openings for stuffing objects in an area where you'll be adding something else (such as a tail on a bunny), or along a straight edge that is easy to slipstitch closed.
- Use the sewing machine setting that is right for the fabric you are sewing. When sewing tricot, set your sewing machine for sewing stretchy fabrics. This allows fabric to stretch without the stitches breaking during play. When sewing vinyl, set machine stitch to a long width, since small stitches can make vinyl tear like a perforated piece of paper.

Getting Ready

Enlarging patterns

Many of the patterns in this book must be enlarged before tracing. You can do this at a photocopy shop, or on some home printers. If the required enlargement is too big for your printer (for example, if the pattern must be enlarged by 400%, and your printer's maximum is 200%) enlarge and print the pattern at 200%, then enlarge the printed pattern by another 200%.

Tracing patterns

Use a fabric pen or tailor's chalk to trace pattern pieces (Figure A).

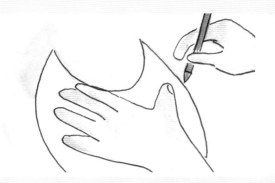

Figure A

Laying out pattern pieces

- In some projects, I recommend folding fabric before cutting the patterns. This allows you to make an identical reverse image of the pattern. It also means you spend less time cutting pattern pieces.
- Some patterns have arrows that indicate how to lay pattern pieces on the fabric. This is important in fabrics with visible fibers, such as tricot and fleece.
- The bias is the diagonal line across the fabric. Fabrics cut on the bias are stretchier and drape well. Bias strips are used for binding fabric edges.
- The selvage is the area of fabric along the edges of both sides of a fabric roll (Figure B). When laying out a pattern, the arrows on the pattern should be aligned with selvage (Figure C).

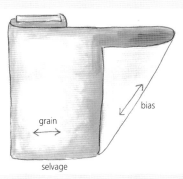

bias

grain

selvage

Figure B

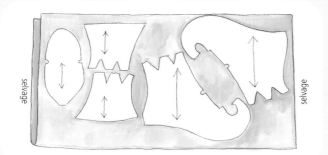

Figure C

Using an iron

It is very important that all fabrics are flat before they are cut and sewn together, so iron fabric before cutting them, if necessary. You'll also need an iron for the following purposes (Figure D):

Figure D

- To iron fabric stabilizer onto the back of fabrics.
- To press darts. Press these on a sleeve board rather than a flat ironing board to achieve the desired curve.
- To press seams. When making blankets and other flat pieces, it is often necessary to press seams open.
- To press finished pieces.
- To steam delicate fabrics. In such cases, you'll need to use a steam iron (Figure E).

Figure E

- To flatten vinyl. Always use a pressing cloth so that you don't melt the vinyl.

Basic Techniques

Quilting

Sewing layers of fabric together with a layer of batting in the center (Figures A, B and C).

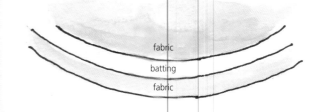

Figure A

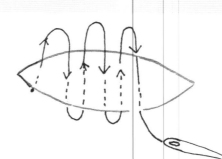

Figure B

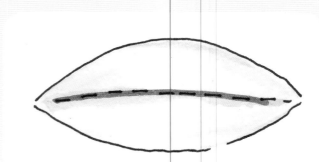

Figure C

Finishing edges

The raw edges of most pieces of fabric will ravel unless they are secured in some way. To finish fabric edges, you can do one of the following:

STEP 1

Sew edges using a special sewing machine called a serger.

STEP 2

Sew edges on zigzag setting with a regular sewing machine.

STEP 3

Cut edges with pinking shears.

Fabrics with edges that do not ravel include felt, fleece, vinyl and leather.

Appliquéing shapes onto fabric

When sewing one piece of fabric onto another, the piece you appliqué should be slightly stiff. This prevents it from wrinkling when it is sewn onto the base fabric.

STEP 1

Iron fabric stabilizer onto back of piece you want to appliqué.

STEP 2

Pin appliqué firmly onto base piece. Make sure pins are placed vertically so that they can be sewn over.

STEP 3

Using the zigzag setting on your sewing machine (make the zigzag close together), sew around appliqué (Figure D). Press.

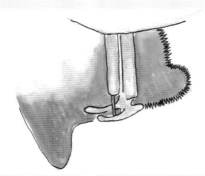

Figure D

Overstitch

This stitch is used to hold down unseen, inner pieces and for decoration. It is also known as a topstitch (Figures E and F).

Figure E

Figure F

Making a simple hem

STEP 1

Make a ¼" (0.6 cm) fold along edge of fabric and iron it. Make a second ¼" (0.6 cm) fold and iron it.

STEP 2

Stitch folds closed near top fold. If you don't want the stitches to be seen, slipstitch the hem by hand (Figure G).

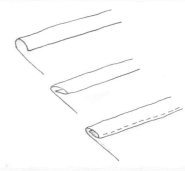

Figure G

Sewing pieces that will be turned right side out

STEP 1

Many projects are sewn together with their wrong sides facing out. When sewing a seam around the project, leave an opening for turning the project right side out.

STEP 2

After the project is sewn, make small cuts in corners and curves. This makes the corners pointier and the curves smoother when the project is turned right side out. Be careful not to cut the seams (Figure H).

Figure H

STEP 3

Turn project right side out. Insert stuffing (if required), then hand-sew the opening closed.

Bias Tape

Bias tape is a strip of fabric that is folded and sewn over edges to give them a clean and decorative finish. Bias tape is cut on a 45° angle, making it stretchy and easy to fold along curves.

Making bias tape

STEP 1

Use a right angle to mark 45°, and a long ruler to measure strips that are 1½" (3.5 cm) wide on the bias of a fabric (Figure I). Cut the strips.

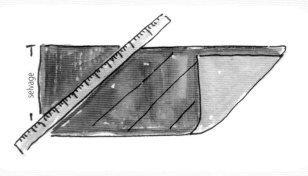

Figure I

STEP 2

Place strips with right sides together, and short ends aligned at a right angle. Sew, then press seam open.

STEP 3

Measure the edges you want to enclose with bias tape and add ½" (1.3 cm) to the amount of bias tape you prepare. When using bias tape for bibs that tie, add about 10" (25.4 cm) of bias tape at each end of bib, to make the ties (Figure J).

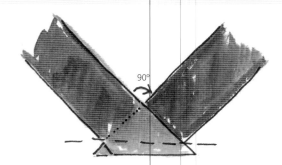

Figure J

Sewing on bias tape

STEP 1

Trim area where bias tape will be sewn about ⅛" (0.3 cm) from the seam. Press open half of the bias tape, and line up raw edge of fabric with unfolded side of bias tape (Figure K).

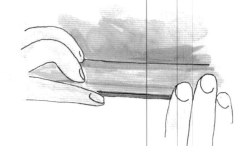

Figure K

STEP 2

Pin right side of bias tape to right side of fabric. Stitch bias tape to fabric, with seam allowance equal to width of presser foot (Figure L).

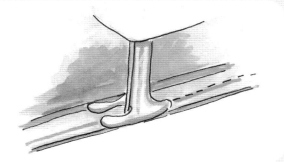

Figure L

STEP 3

Fold bias tape in half so that it almost touches the edge of the object you are sewing (Figure M).

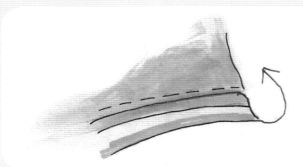

Figure M

STEP 4

Fold bias tape over again so that it is folded over the edge of the fabric.

STEP 5

Sew along bias tape, near outer edge (Figure N).

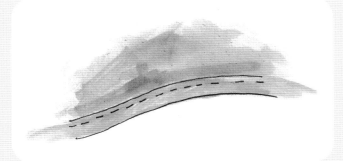

Figure N

STEP 6

To finish, cross beginning and end pieces of bias tape, and sew down. Press.

Making shanks

A shank makes the area between two separate pieces stronger. Shanks are required in areas where a button is added to a garment, an arm is sewn onto a doll, or a wing is attached to a duck. To make a shank, do the following:

STEP 1

Insert a knotted piece of thread near the joint and make a small stitch.

STEP 2

Wrap thread around the joint four or five times, then knot the thread and cut (Figure O).

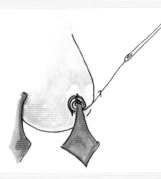

Figure O

Making gathers and ruffles

STEP 1

Using heavy thread, sew two lines of wide stitches across fabric edge. (Make three lines of wide stitches if piece is very long.)

STEP 2

Each stitch consists of an upper and lower thread. Knot the thread on one side. Take threads (top or bottom) on other side and gently pull at the same time.

STEP 3

Gently adjust gathers with your fingers, pulling them evenly across the fabric edge (Figure P).

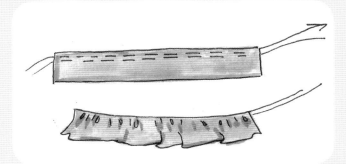

Figure P

Sewing decorative piping

Piping is a decorative trim sewn between two seams.

STEP 1

Line up raw edge of piping with raw edge of fabric, on right side of fabric. The decorative, round part of the piping should be on the fabric. Using a zipper foot, sew piping all along the raw edge (Figures Q and R).

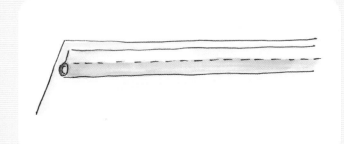

Figure Q

Figure R

STEP 2

Sew along pre-sewn stitch on piping (Figure S).

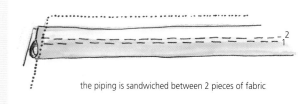

the piping is sandwiched between 2 pieces of fabric

Figure S

STEP 3

Place the other half of the project fabric on top of the piping, right side down. Sew above the first stitch.

STEP 4

Finish piping by overlapping the two ends (Figure T).

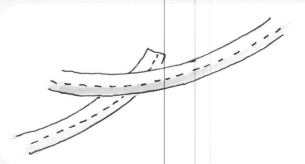

Figure T

STEP 5

When you unfold the fabric, the decorative piping will be between them.

Sewing scalloped edges

Carefully snip scalloped edges at regular intervals on curves and in the corners between the curves, so that when the fabric is turned right side out, the curves are smooth. When snipping curves and corners, take care not to cut the seam (Figure U).

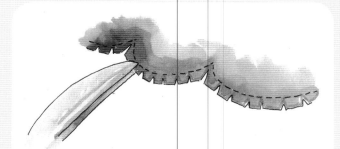

Figure U

Sewing vinyl

- Put a layer of sheer tissue paper over and under vinyl before sewing.
- The tissue paper allows the presser foot to slide over the vinyl, making an even stitch. Tear the paper away after you've finished sewing.
- Set your machine stitch to a long width when sewing with vinyl.
- Small stitches tend to cut the vinyl, making it tear like a perforated piece of paper at the line of stitching.
- Iron vinyl to eliminate wrinkles by placing a pressing cloth (a piece of cotton is fine) between the vinyl and the iron. Don't leave the iron on the pressing cloth too long. Direct contact with an iron will melt vinyl.
- Use a special plastic presser foot made for sewing vinyl and foam (Figure V).

Figure V

Cutting fabric with a nap

Fabrics such as faux fur and velvet have a nap. Pattern pieces should be placed on the fabric so that the nap is going down. If you fold the fabric, fold it vertically so that the nap on both sides of the fold goes the same way (Figures W and X).

Figure W

Figure X

Faux fur should not be folded before cutting. Each piece should be cut separately so that each piece is exact. When cutting faux fur, cut through the weave on the back of the fur, and take care not to cut the fur itself. When two pieces of faux fur are sewn together, the fur will get caught in the seam. Use a needle to draw the fur out of the seam.

Stuffing sewn objects

When sewing an object that will be stuffed, leave a small opening along a straight area of the object's seam for inserting stuffing or batting.

STEP 1

Take a handful of stuffing (less if it is meant for a very small area) and tuck it into the opening. Use a chopstick, dowel rod, or the end of a paint brush to firmly push the stuffing into the toy (Figure Y).

Figure Y

STEP 2

If there are arms, legs, or other appendages, stuff these first. Then stuff the head and body.

STEP 3

Continue stuffing the toy until it is firm to the touch. Slipstitch the opening to close. Press or steam, as instructed.

Farm Animal Fabric Puzzle

This puzzle is great for babies, since it's soft, pretty, and fun to look at. It's easy to fold up and carry, thanks to the inclusion of handles and tying ribbons. Just fold the puzzle board, with the pieces inside, and carry it like a bag. I recommend using fabric with different textures for each animal so that the board is both tactilely and visually interesting.

EXPERIENCE LEVEL

DIMENSIONS
- Open: 24" x 32" (61.0 cm x 81.3 cm)
- Folded: 12" x 32" (30.5 cm x 81.3 cm)

MATERIALS
Puzzle board
- 21" x 29" (53.5 cm x 73.7 cm) piece of iron-on fabric stabilizer, medium weight
- 21" x 29" (53.3 cm x 73.7 cm) piece of light blue felt (for puzzle board top)
- 24" x 33" (61 cm x 83.8 cm) piece of striped denim (for puzzle board base bottom)
- 24" x 33" (61 cm x 83.8 cm) piece of polka dot cotton fabric (for puzzle board base top)
- 8" x 10" (20.3 cm x 25.4 cm) piece of pink cotton fabric (for pig)
- 9" x 10" (22.9 cm x 25.4 cm) piece of yellow cotton fabric (for duck)
- 9" x 11" (22.9 cm x 27.9 cm) piece of brown cotton fabric (for horse)
- 8" x 11" (20.3 cm x 27.9 cm) piece of orange cotton fabric (for rooster)
- 9" x 10" (22.9 cm x 25.4 cm) piece of white cotton fabric (for rabbit)
- 10" x 10" (25.4 cm x 25.4 cm) piece of beige cotton fabric (for sheep)
- Matching sewing thread (pink, yellow, beige, orange, brown, white)
- Two 28" (71.1 cm) pieces of blue ribbon, 2" (5.1 cm) wide (for handles)
- Four 8" (20.3 cm) pieces of plastic boning (for handles)
- Ten 12" (30.5 cm) pieces of red ribbon, ½" (1.3 cm) wide (for closing puzzle)

Stuffed animals
- 10" x 17" (25.4 cm x 43.2 cm) piece of yellow fabric (for duck body and rooster beak)
- 11" x 17" (27.9 cm x 43.2 cm) piece of orange fabric (for duck bill and rooster body)
- 4" x 4" (10.2 cm x 10.2 cm) piece of red cotton fabric (for rooster comb)
- 9" x 21" (22.9 cm x 53.3 cm) piece of brown fabric (for horse body)
- 11" x 16" (27.9 cm x 48.3 cm) piece of white wool fabric (for bunny body)
- 4" x 4" (10.2 cm x 10.2 cm) piece of pink felt (for bunny ears)
- 10" x 19" (25.4 cm x 48.3 cm) piece of beige faux fur (for sheep body)
- 4" x 4" (10.2 cm x 10.2 cm) piece of black wool fabric (for sheep ears and muzzle)
- 10" x 13" (25.4 cm x 33.0 cm) piece of satin pink fabric (for pig body)
- Matching sewing thread (yellow, orange, red, brown, white, pink, beige, black)
- Polyester fiberfill stuffing
- 2½" x 2½" (6.5 cm x 6.5 cm) piece of marabou (for bunny tail)
- 40" (101.6 cm) piece of brown yarn (for pony mane and tail)
- Black and pink embroidery thread (for eyes and mouths)

TOOLS
- Embroidery needle
- Fabric pen or tailor's chalk
- Iron
- Pins
- Scissors
- Sewing machine
- Sewing needle

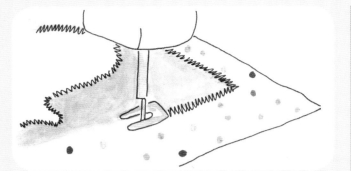

Figure A

Figure B

Getting Started

• Copy Farm Animal Fabric Puzzle Pattern pieces (pages 108-109), and cut.

Puzzle board

• Iron fabric stabilizer onto back of felt. Trace Board Top pattern onto blue felt, and cut.

• Pin striped denim and polka dot cotton fabric together. Trace Board Bottom pattern, and cut.

• Trace Board Rooster, Board Pony, Board Bunny, Board Pig, Board Duck, and Board Sheep patterns onto appropriate pieces of cotton fabric, and cut.

Stuffed animals

• Fold yellow fabric, and pin. Trace Duck and Rooster Beak patterns, and cut.

• Fold orange fabric, and pin. Trace Duck Bill and Rooster patterns, and cut.

• Fold red fabric, and pin. Trace Rooster Comb pattern, and cut.

• Fold brown fabric, and pin. Trace Pony pattern, and cut.

• Fold white fabric, and pin. Trace Bunny pattern, and cut.

• Fold pink fabric, and pin. Trace Bunny Inner Ear pattern, and cut.

• Fold beige fabric, and pin. Trace Sheep pattern, and cut.

• Fold black fabric, and pin. Trace Sheep Muzzle and Ear patterns, and cut.

• Fold pink fabric, and pin. Trace Pig pattern, and cut.

Instructions

Puzzle board

STEP 1

Pin animal board pieces onto board top piece. Zigzag around each piece with matching thread.

STEP 2

Center felt board top piece onto polka dot board bottom piece, and pin. Zigzag all around with matching thread (Figures A and B).

STEP 3

For handles, fold blue ribbon in half vertically, and pin. Make two 90° folds in ribbon, 9½" (24.1 cm) from each end, and pin. Slide 2 pieces of plastic boning into each handle. Stitch ribbon closed, along bottom.

STEP 4

Pin handles onto polka dot board bottom piece (see pattern marking), and lay handles on top of board.

STEP 5

For ties, pin red ribbons onto edge of polka dot board bottom piece (see pattern marking), and lay ribbons on top of board.

STEP 6

Sew a seam all around puzzle board, close to the edge, to secure handles and ribbons (Figure C).

STEP 7

Place denim board bottom piece on top of polka dot board bottom piece, right sides together. Make sure all ribbons and handles are sandwiched between the two layers, away from area to be sewn (Figure D).

STEP 8

Sew a seam all around edge of puzzle, leaving an opening for turning puzzle right side out.

STEP 9

Turn puzzle right side out, and press. Overstitch around outer edge of puzzle to secure handles and ties, and close opening. Press (Figure E).

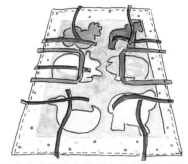

Figure C

Figure D

Figure E

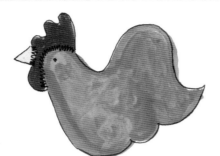

Figure F

Figure G

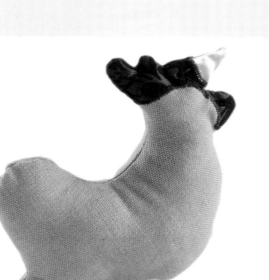

Stuffed animals

Rooster

STEP 1

Pin each beak piece to a comb piece. Zigzag at base of beaks with matching thread. Pin each comb piece to a rooster piece. Zigzag at base of comb with matching thread. (Figure F).

STEP 2

Pin right sides of rooster pieces together. Sew a seam all around, leaving a small opening for turning right side out.

STEP 3

Turn rooster right side out. Insert stuffing, then slipstitch opening to close. Press.

STEP 4

Embroider a French knot on each side, for eyes.

Pony

STEP 1

To make tail, make several loops in a piece of yarn, then stitch the ends together. Repeat to make the mane and bangs.

STEP 2

Pin tail, mane, and bangs onto one pony piece (see pattern marking), and stitch down (Figure G).

STEP 3

Pin pony pieces, right sides together. Make sure loops of yarn are sandwiched between pieces, so that they aren't caught in the seam when bodies are sewn together.

STEP 4

Sew a seam all around, leaving a small opening on the belly for turning right side out.

STEP 5

Turn pony right side out. Insert stuffing, then slipstitch opening to close. Press.

STEP 6

Embroider a French knot on each side, for eyes.

Figure H

Bunny

STEP 1

Pin each inner ear piece to a bunny piece (see pattern marking). Zigzag around inner ear with matching thread (Figure H).

STEP 2

Pin bunny pieces, right sides together. Sew a seam all around, leaving a small opening near the tail for turning right side out.

STEP 3

Turn bunny right side out. Insert stuffing, then slipstitch opening to close. Press.

STEP 4

Sew a piece of marabou at opening, for the tail.

STEP 5

Embroider a French knot on each side, for eyes, and a nose with backstitch.

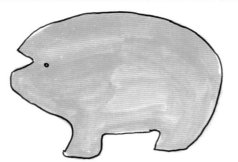

Figure I

Figure J

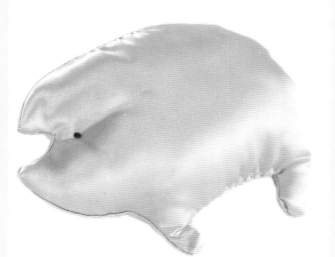

Pig

STEP 1

Pin pig pieces, right sides together. Sew a seam all around, leaving a small opening for turning right side out.

STEP 2

Turn pig right side out. Insert stuffing, then slipstitch opening to close. Press.

STEP 3

Embroider a French knot on each side, for eyes (Figure I).

Duck

STEP 1

Pin each bill piece to a duck piece. Zigzag at base of bill with matching thread (Figure J).

STEP 2

Pin duck pieces, right sides together. Sew a seam all around, leaving a small opening for turning right side out.

STEP 3

Turn duck right side out. Insert stuffing, then slipstitch opening to close. Press.

STEP 4

Embroider a French knot on each side, for eyes.

Sheep

STEP 1

Pin each ear and muzzle piece to a sheep piece (Figure K). Zigzag around ears with matching thread.

STEP 2

Pin sheep pieces, right sides together. Sew a seam all around, leaving a small opening for turning right side out.

STEP 3

Turn sheep right side out. Insert stuffing, then slipstitch opening to close. Press.

STEP 4

Embroider a French knot on each side, for eyes, and a mouth with backstitch.

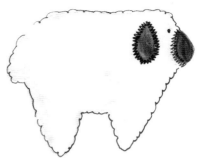

Figure K

Mama and Baby Duck

I loved ducks when I was a girl, and even had pet ducks that I often played with. When my youngest daughter was born, a dear childhood friend gave her a stuffed duck as a present. Today, my daughter has more than 20 different ducks in her collection. I made this Mama and Baby Duck pair with her collection in mind. They will appeal to any child who loves soft, fluffy ducks. They also make lovely room decorations!

EXPERIENCE LEVEL

DIMENSIONS
• Mama duck: 13" x 18" (33 cm x 45.7 cm)
• Baby duck: 7" x 8" (12.7 cm x 20.3 cm)

MATERIALS
• 36" x 21" (91.4 cm x 50.8 cm) piece of white tricot fabric (for one mama)
• 10" x 16" (25.4 cm x 40.6 cm) piece of yellow tricot fabric (for one baby)
• 13" x 14" (33 cm x 35.6 cm) piece of orange felt (for bill and feet on each)
• Polyester fiberfill batting (for wings)
• Polyester fiberfill stuffing (for body)
• Matching sewing thread (yellow, white, orange)
• Blue embroidery thread (for eyes)

TOOLS
• Doll needle
• Embroidery needle
• Fabric pen
• Pin
• Safety pin
• Scissors
• Sewing machine
• Sewing needle

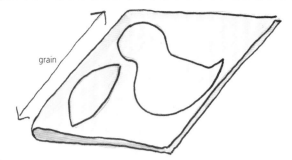

Figure A

Figure B

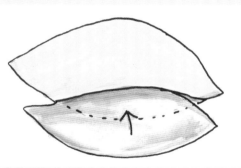

Figure C

Getting Started

• Copy Mama and Baby Duck Pattern pieces (pages 110 and 111), and cut.

• Fold white tricot in half, and pin. With tricot fibers running vertically, trace Mama Duck and Mama Duck Wing patterns on fabric, and cut.

• Fold yellow tricot in half, and pin. With fibers running vertically, trace Baby Duck and Baby Duck Wing patterns, and cut.

• Trace Baby Duck Wing and Mama Duck Wing patterns onto batting, and cut.

• Fold orange felt in half, and pin. Trace Baby Duck Foot, Baby Duck Bill, Mama Duck Foot, and Mama Duck Bill patterns, and cut.

Instructions

> Follow same instructions for Mama Duck and Baby Duck.

STEP 1

Pin bill pieces together, right sides together. Sew a seam along rounded edges, leaving straight edge open for turning right side out. Turn bill right side out, and insert stuffing.

STEP 2

Pin pairs of foot pieces together, wrong sides together. Sew a seam around entire foot, then fold leg part in half vertically, and hand-sew (folded leg will be too thick to machine sew) (Figure B).

STEP 3

Set sewing machine for sewing stretchy fabrics. (This setting allows tricot to stretch during play and keeps stitches from breaking.) Pin pairs of wing pieces, right sides together. Sew a seam all around, leaving an opening for turning right side out.

STEP 4

Turn wing right side out, and insert batting (Figure C).

STEP 5

Pin body pieces, right sides together. Sew a seam all around, leaving an opening at bottom for turning right side out (Figure D).

STEP 6

Turn body right side out. Insert stuffing until firmly stuffed, then slipstitch opening to close.

STEP 7

With matching thread, use a small slipstitch to hand-sew bill onto body (Figure E).

STEP 8

Sew legs onto body (see pattern marking), using a long doll needle and embroidery thread. Sew back and forth through body, sewing from one leg to the other, until legs are firmly attached. To finish sewing on legs, loop the thread three or four times around each leg, where leg meets body, to make a shank for each leg. Finish with a knot (Figures F and G).

STEP 9

Sew wings onto body (see pattern marking) using a long doll needle. Sew back and forth through duck body and wings. To finish, loop the thread three or four times around each wing, where wing meets duck body, making a shank for each wing. Finish with a knot. (Sewing the wings onto the body this way allows you to move the wings as you like.)

STEP 10

Embroider a French knot on each side, for eyes.

Figure D

Figure E

Figure F

Figure G

Fun and Fresh Groceries and Bag

Though children are usually told not to play with their food, that's exactly what they should do when its made with vibrantly-colored, fun-to-touch fabrics! This project features a soft felt grocery bag and plenty of fruits and vegetables. Children love touching and rolling the fruit as well as filling and emptying the grocery bag. It can also be used to play a lively game of Going to the Supermarket!

EXPERIENCE LEVEL

DIMENSIONS

- Grocery bag: 11" x 8" x 6" (27.9 cm x 20.3 cm x 15.2 cm)
- Apple: 6" x 12" (15.2 cm x 30.5 cm)
- Carrot: 7" x 14" (17.8 cm x 35.6 cm)
- Potato: 7" x 8" (17.8 cm x 15.2 cm)
- Pear: 7" x 11" (17.8 cm x 27.9 cm)
- Strawberry: 4" x 6" (10.2 cm x 15.2 cm)
- Banana: 4½" x 6" (11.4 cm x 15.2 cm)
- Orange: 7" x 13" (17.8 cm x 33.0 cm)

MATERIALS

- 20" x 30" (50.8 cm x 76.2 cm) piece of iron-on fabric stabilizer, medium weight
- 20" x 30" (50.8 cm x 76.2 cm) piece of beige felt (for grocery bag)
- 7" x 14" (18.5 cm x 35.6 cm) piece of red cotton fabric (for apple)
- 13" x 12" (33.0 cm x 30.5 cm) piece of orange terry cloth (for orange)
- 6" x 7" (15.2 cm x 17.8 cm) beige tricot fabric (for potato)
- 15" x 8" (38.1 cm x 20.3 cm) piece of light green cotton fabric (for pear)
- 10" x 5" (25.4 cm x 12.7 cm) piece of red or pink cotton fabric (for strawberry)
- 10" x 11" (25.4 cm x 27.9 cm) piece of striped orange cotton fabric (for carrot)
- 25" x 14" (63.5 cm x 35.6 cm) piece of green cotton fabric (for small leaves, large leaves and carrot top)

- 9" x 9" (23 cm x 23 cm) piece of cream cotton fabric (for banana)
- 9" x 9" (23 cm x 23 cm) piece of yellow satin fabric (for banana)
- 9" x 9" (23 cm x 23 cm) piece of white cotton fabric (for banana)
- Polyester fiberfill stuffing (for stuffing fruits and vegetables)
- Polyester fiberfill batting (for stuffing leaves)
- Matching sewing thread (beige/brown, cream, red, yellow, orange, green, pink)
- Embroidery thread (beige, yellow, black, green)

TOOLS

- Chopstick
- Embroidery needle
- Iron
- Marking pen or tailor's chalk
- Pinking shears
- Pins
- Safety pin
- Scissors
- Sewing needle

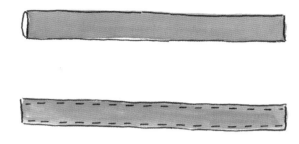

Figure A

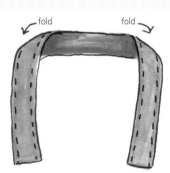

Figure B

Figure C

Getting Started

• Copy Fun and Fresh Groceries and Bag Pattern pieces (pages 112-114), and cut.

Bag

• Iron fabric stabilizer onto back of beige felt. Fold felt in half, right sides together.
• Trace Bag Front/Back pattern, and cut.
• Trace Bag Handle pattern, and cut.
• Trace Bag Side pattern, and cut.

Fruits and Vegetables

• Trace Apple pattern onto red fabric, and cut.
• Trace Orange pattern onto orange terry cloth, and cut.
• Trace Potato pattern onto beige tricot, and cut.
• Trace Pear pattern onto light green fabric, and cut.
• Trace Strawberry pattern onto pink or red fabric, and cut.
• Trace Carrot pattern onto striped orange cotton, and cut.
• Trace Carrot Top pattern onto green felt, and cut.
• Trace Banana Fruit patterns onto cream fabric, and cut.
• Trace Yellow Banana Peel patterns onto yellow fabric, and cut.
• Trace White Banana Peel patterns onto white fabric, and cut.
• Trace Big Leaf and Small Leaf patterns onto green fabrics and batting, and cut.
• Trace Strawberry Leaf pattern onto green fabric, and cut.

Instructions

Bag

STEP 1

Fold each handle piece in half lengthwise, and press. Sew a seam along long raw edge. Do not sew ends (Figure A).

STEP 2

Attach a safety pin to one end of each handle, then draw safety pin through fabric tunnel to turn handle right side out.

STEP 3

Make a 90° fold at each end of each handle, 4½" (11.5 cm) from the end, and press (Figure B).

STEP 4

Pin bag front pieces together, with right sides (felt sides) together. Pin bag back and bag side pieces together in same manner.

STEP 5

Pin handles to bag front and bag back pieces (see pattern marking). Sew on handles by topstitching a rectangle.

STEP 6

Pin bag side pieces to bag front and bag back pieces, right sides together. Sew along three sides, leaving top open (Figure C).

STEP 7

Trim seams on inside of bag, about ⅛" (0.3 cm) from seam.

STEP 8

To finish top of bag, cut top edge with pinking shears. Turn bag right side out and press (Figure D).

STEP 9

To form creases in bag sides, tuck in sides, flatten front and back, and press (Figure E).

Fruits and Vegetables
Potato
STEP 1

Set sewing machine for sewing stretchy fabrics. Pin potato pieces, right sides together (Figure F). Sew a seam all around, leaving an opening for turning right side out.

STEP 2

Turn potato right side out. Insert stuffing, then slipstitch opening to close.

STEP 3

To make indentations for potato eyes, use beige or brown embroidery thread. Knot one end of thread and insert needle into one side of potato, pushing it through the potato and drawing it out through other side. Pull gently on thread, then tie a knot close to potato surface. Insert needle into potato, close to the knot, and draw through to the other side. Pull gently to make indentation, then tie a knot.

STEP 4

Repeat to make several indentations so that the potato looks lumpy and authentic (Figure G).

Figure D

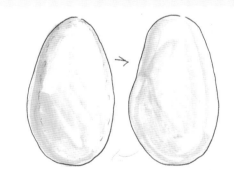

Figure E

Figure F

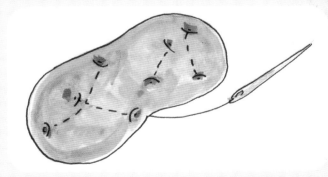

Figure G

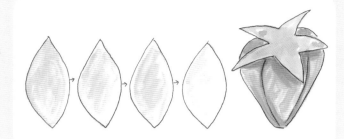

Figure H

Figure I

Figure J

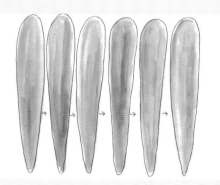

Figure K

Apple/Pear/Strawberry/Orange

STEP 1

Pin apple (pear/strawberry/orange) pieces together, one beside the other, to make a closed shape (Figures H and I).

STEP 2

Sew pieces together, leaving a small opening along one side for turning fruit right side out.

STEP 3

Turn fruit right side out. Insert stuffing, then slipstitch opening to close.

STEP 4

For apple and pear: Hand-sew a leaf at top (Figure J).

STEP 5

For strawberry: Embroider short yellow lines all over, and hand-sew strawberry leaf on top.

STEP 6

For orange: Embroider a black navel on the top using backstitch.

Carrot

STEP 1

Pin carrot pieces together, one after the other, to form a closed shape. Sew pieces together, leaving top of shape open for inserting carrot tops (Figure K).

STEP 2

Turn carrot right side out and insert with stuffing. Use a chopstick to push stuffing firmly into bottom point.

STEP 3

Pin pairs of carrot top pieces, right sides together. Sew a seam on three sides, leaving one short side open (Figure L).

STEP 4

Attach safety pin to the unsewn short side, and draw through inside of carrot top to turn it right side out.

STEP 5

Insert stuffing, using a chopstick to push it firmly into each carrot top. Slipstitch opening to close.

STEP 6

Hand-sew the bottoms of three or four carrots tops together (Figure M).

STEP 7

Insert bottom of carrot top into open end of carrot (Figure N).

STEP 8

Make a running stitch around edge of carrot, then pull thread to gather top of carrot closed (Figure O).

STEP 9

Make several stitches around top of carrot to secure carrot tops inside (Figure P). Wrap embroidery thread around base of carrot tops for extra support.

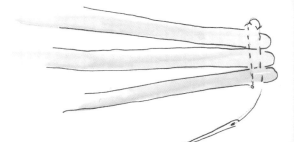

Figure M

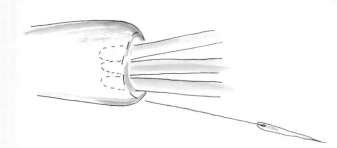

Figure N

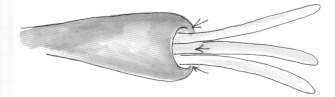

Figure O

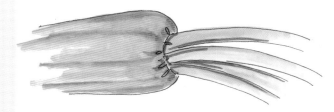

Figure P

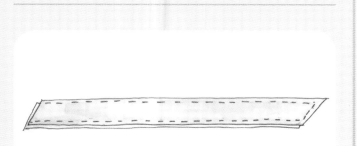

Figure L

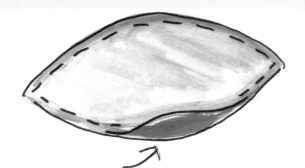

Figure Q

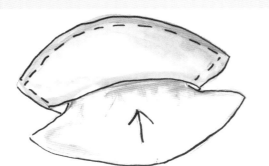

Figure R

Figure S

Leaves

STEP 1

Pin pairs of leaf pieces, right sides together. Sew a seam all around, leaving an opening for turning right side out (Figure Q).

STEP 2

For big leaf/small leaf, turn leaf right side out, and insert batting (Figure R).

STEP 3

Quilt a leaf pattern onto each leaf (Figure S). Press.

STEP 4

For strawberry leaf, turn strawberry leaf piece right side out, and insert stuffing. Use a chopstick to poke stuffing into pointy tips of leaf.

STEP 5

Hand-sew the leaves onto the fruits.

Banana

STEP 1

Pin banana fruit pieces together, one after another, to form a closed shape. Be sure to match up notches (see pattern marking). Sew A to B, AB to C, ABC to D, and ABCD to A. Leave a small hole in one seam, near the bottom, for turning banana right side out (Figure T).

STEP 2

Turn banana fruit right side out, and insert stuffing. Slipstitch opening to close.

STEP 3

Pin yellow banana peel pieces together, one after another. Be sure to match up notches. Sew A to B, AB to C, ABC to D, and ABCD to A. Sew seams along bottoms, up to notches.

STEP 4

Pin white banana peel pieces together in the same manner as yellow peel pieces, and sew (Figure U).

STEP 5

Put right sides of yellow and white peels together, and sew a seam around upper part of shape. Leave an opening for turning peel right side out.

STEP 6

Turn right side out, and slipstitch opening to close. Press. Hand-sew lining and peel together at the bottom. Put fruit into peel.

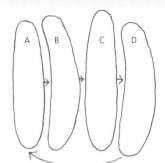

Figure T

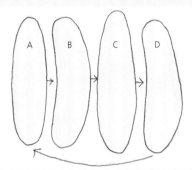

Figure U

Crinkly Goldfish Toy

Babies like toys that make sounds and thanks to the use of crinkly plastic (use the bag that holds cereal inside the box, or the plastic used in packages of baby wipes), this toy makes a fantastic sound. I used a variety of fabric textures for this fish, so that it's also interesting for babies to touch. The fins are made from satin and the tail is chiffon. The body is made from quilted batting-lined satin, giving it a three-dimensional look and feel.

EXPERIENCE LEVEL

DIMENSIONS

• 7½" x 18½" (18.5 cm x 47 cm)

MATERIALS

• 16" x 16" (40.6 cm x 40.6 cm) piece of orange polyester satin (for body and top fin)

• 7" x 11" (17.8 cm x 27.9 cm) piece of iron-on fabric stabilizer, medium weight

• 24" x 18" (61 cm x 45.7 cm) piece of polyester fiberfill batting (for body and top fin)

• 21" x 12" (53.3 cm x 30.5 cm) piece of orange chiffon (for tail and side fins)

• 5" x 3" (12.7 cm x 7.6 cm) piece of white cotton fabric or vinyl (for eyes)

• 2" x 3" (5.1 cm x 7.6 cm) piece of black cotton fabric or vinyl (for eyes)

• Polyester fiberfill stuffing (for body)

• Matching sewing thread (orange, black, white)

• Crackly plastic (such as the bag in a cereal box or the packaging for baby wipes)

TOOLS

• Fabric pen
• Iron
• Pins
• Scissors
• Sewing machine
• Sewing needle

Figure A

Figure B

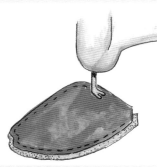

Figure C

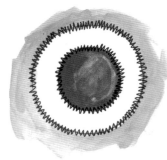

Figure D

Getting Started

For this project, mark patterns on satin first, then iron fabric stabilizer on back of pattern pieces that need it. After that, cut all the pieces at the same time.

• Copy Crinkly Goldfish Toy Pattern pieces (page 115), and cut.

• Fold satin in half, and pin. Trace Top Fin, Side Fin, and Body patterns onto satin.

• Iron fabric stabilizer on back of Body patterns. Cut out patterns.

• Trace Top Fin and Body patterns onto batting, and cut.

• Fold chiffon in half, and pin. Trace Tail pattern, and cut.

• Trace Outer Eye pattern onto white vinyl, and cut.

• Trace Inner Eye pattern onto black vinyl, and cut.

Instructions

STEP 1

Pin top fin pieces, right sides together. Sew a seam along three sides, leaving bottom open.

STEP 2

Turn fin inside out and insert batting. Quilt fin by sewing vertical lines across it (Figure A). Press.

STEP 3

Pin side fin pieces, right sides together. Sew a seam along three sides, leaving bottom open.

STEP 4

Turn fin inside out and insert batting. Quilt fin by sewing vertical line across.

STEP 5

Pin tail pieces, right sides together. Sew a seam around curved edge of tail, leaving straight edge unsewn, for gathers (see pattern marking). Since chiffon frays easily, zigzag the seamed edges.

STEP 6

Turn tail right side out, and press. Insert batting, and quilt by sewing vertical lines across it. Make gathers along unsewn edge of tail

STEP 7

Place body pieces made from batting on wrong side of satin body pieces, and pin. Sew a seam all around each piece, very close to the edge (Figure C).

STEP 8

To make eyes, zigzag inner eye piece onto outer eye piece with matching thread. Zigzag outer eye piece onto fish body (see pattern marking) with matching thread (Figure D).

STEP 9

Lay scales pattern onto body pieces and mark with fabric pen. Quilt scales by stitching along marked lines (Figure E).

STEP 10

Zigzag side fin pieces onto body pieces (see pattern marking) (Figure F).

STEP 11

Place tail at end of one fish body, with gathered end aligned with fish end, and other end of tail facing fish front. Stitch down tail (Figure G).

STEP 12

Place top fin at top of one body piece, with top of fin facing down and raw edges lined up. Stitch down fin (Figure H).

STEP 13

Place body pieces together, right sides together. Make sure tail is sandwiched between body pieces and not in the area where seams will be sewn. Sew a seam all around, leaving an opening for turning fish right side out.

STEP 14

Turn fish right side out. Insert pieces of crackly paper inside fish, and press up against fish sides. Insert stuffing between pieces of crackly paper, then slipstitch opening to close. Press.

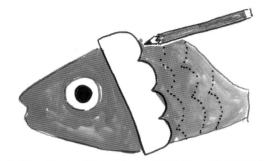

Figure E

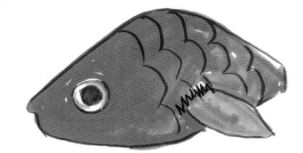

Figure F

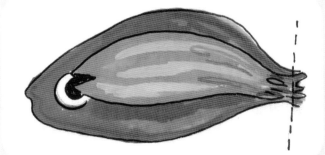

Figure G

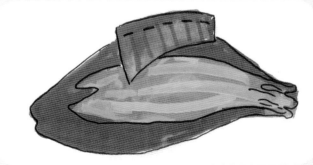

Figure H

Velcro® Peelable Banana

As a baby, my eldest daughter had a favorite hat that fastened with Velcro®. She kept herself occupied for hours, simply pulling apart the Velcro® and sticking it back together again, over and over again. That hat inspired me to make this Velcro® banana, which keeps little hands busy with its familiar shape and fantastic sound.

EXPERIENCE LEVEL

DIMENSIONS

• 6½" x 7" (16.5 cm x 17.8 cm)

MATERIALS

• 7" x 8" (17.8 cm x 20.3 cm) piece of thick yellow vinyl (for peel)
• 2" x 28" (5.1 cm x 71.1 cm) piece of white Velcro®
• Matching sewing thread (yellow, white)

TOOLS

• Embroidery needle
• Pins
• Pressing cloth (for pressing vinyl)
• Scissors
• Sewing machine with presser foot made for vinyl
• Small pliers (for pulling needle through vinyl)
• Tailor's chalk
• Thimble

Velcro® has a stiff side and a soft side. Use the stiff side to make the peel and the soft side to make the fruit.

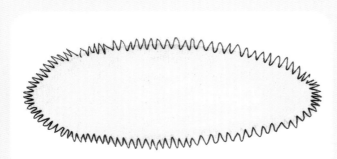

Figure A

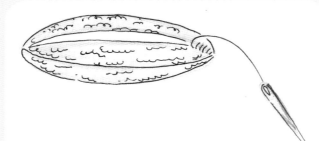

Figure B

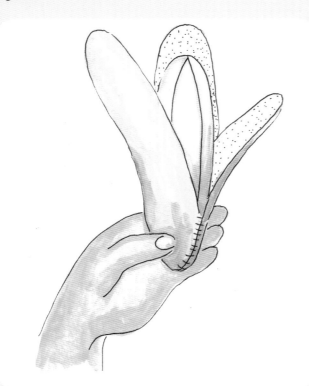

Figure C

Getting Started

- Copy Velcro® Peelable Banana Pattern pieces (page 114), and cut.
- Copy Peel pattern onto vinyl and stiff side of Velcro®, and cut.
- Copy Fruit pattern onto soft side of Velcro®, and cut.

Instructions

STEP 1

Pin each vinyl peel piece to a Velcro® peel piece, wrong sides together. With a presser foot made for vinyl and matching thread, zigzag all around. Make sure needle goes over edge of both Velcro® and vinyl. Zigzag twice around each shape (Figure A).

STEP 2

Fold each peel piece in half, Velcro® sides together. Using a pressing cloth, press peel so that it folds gently.

STEP 3

Pin fruit pieces together, one beside the other. With wrong side facing, sew three sides together, leaving the fourth side open. (Velcro® is very stiff and you won't be able to turn it right side out if you only leave a small hole, so it is important to leave an entire fourth side open).

STEP 4

Turn fruit right side out. Insert stuffing, then hand-sew open side twice to close (Figure B).

STEP 5

Affix peel pieces all around fruit. Sew seams along bottom 2" (5.1 cm) of peel, to connect bottom (Figure C).

Rattling Sheep Ball

This sheep rattle is easy for little hands to pick up and play with. It's a great crib toy, since you'll know your baby is awake when you hear the sound of the rattle. This pattern can also be used to make a soft, fuzzy pillow. Just double the size of the pattern when you copy it, and omit the rattle.

EXPERIENCE LEVEL

DIMENSIONS

• 17" (43.2 cm)

MATERIALS

• 19" x 12" (48.3 cm x 30.5 cm) piece of white faux fur (for ball)
• 3" x 3" (7.6 cm x 7.6 cm) piece of black cotton fabric (for ears, tail, leg, and head)
• 6" x 6" (15.2 cm x 15.2 cm) piece of muslin (for enclosing rattle)
• Matching strong sewing thread (black, white)
• Polyester fiberfill stuffing
• Durable rattle
• Blue embroidery thread (for eyes)

TOOLS

• Embroidery needle
• Fabric pen
• Pins
• Scissors
• Sewing machine
• Sewing needle

Faux fur is quite thick, so always cut it in a single layer.

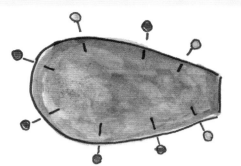

Figure A

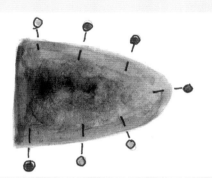

Figure B

Figure C

Be sure to use durable sewing thread when stitching the rattle into the muslin, and the muslin into the body. The muslin creates a pouch for the rattle, so that even if it works its way out of the ball, it will still be enclosed and protected from baby's curious fingers.

Getting Started

- Copy Rattling Sheep Ball Pattern pieces (page 116), and cut.
- Lay faux fur right side down, with nap downwards.
- Trace each Body pattern separately, and cut.
- Fold black cotton in half, and pin. Trace Ear, Tail, Leg and Head patterns, and cut.

Instructions

STEP 1

Pin leg pieces, right sides together. Sew a seam all around, leaving an opening for turning right side out. Turn legs right side out, and press.

STEP 2

Pin pairs of ear pieces, right sides together. Sew a seam all around, leaving an opening for turning right side out. Turn ears right side out, and press (Figure A).

STEP 3

Pin head pieces, right sides together. Sew a seam all around, leaving an opening along the straight edge for turning right side out. Turn right side out, and press.

STEP 4

Fold each ear in half, and stitch along top to secure the fold. Place one ear on each side of head, with open part of ear to the front. Insert a bit of stuffing into the head, then stitch an ear on either side of the head (Figure C).

STEP 5

Place head with ears along one side of a body piece (Figure D).

STEP 6

Pin and sew body pieces, right sides together, in the following order (Figure E).

STEP 7

Pin #1 and #2, with one leg in the seam, and sew. Pin #3 to #2-1, with second leg in the seam, and sew. Pin #4 to #3-2-1, with tail in the seam, and sew. Pin #5 to #4-3-2-1, with third leg in the seam. Sew, leaving an opening for turning ball right side out. Pin #6 to #5-4-3-2-1, with fourth leg in the seam, and sew. Pin #6 to #1, with head and ears in the seam, and sew. You will now have a ball shape with head, ears, legs, and tail on the inside.

STEP 8

Turn ball right side out (Figure F).

Figure D

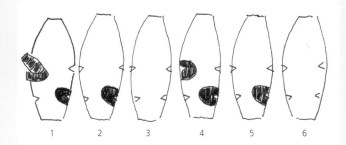

Figure E

Figure F

Figure G

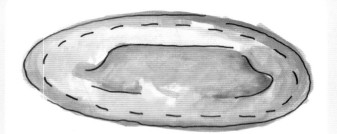

Figure H

Figure I

STEP 9

Fold muslin fabric in half, and cut 2 circles that are large enough to enclose the rattle. Sandwich rattle between muslin pieces, and sew a seam all around. (Figures G and H).

STEP 10

Hand-sew pouch with rattle inside sheep body, using strong sewing thread.

STEP 11

Insert some stuffing into the ball, place rattle on top of stuffing, then continue stuffing ball until firm. Slipstitch opening to close (FigureI).

STEP 12

Embroider French knots, for eyes.

Soft and Funky Building Shapes

Teach your baby shapes and colors with these soft toy shapes. You can make one of every shape, or several of the same shape, but using different funky patterns. To make same shapes of different sizes, alter the size in which you photocopy the pattern. In my experience, the ball seems to be a favorite shape, so make more than one!

EXPERIENCE LEVEL

DIMENSIONS

• Ball: 17½" (44.5 cm)
• Cube: 9" x 9" x 9" (22.9 cm x 22.9 cm x 22.9 cm)
• Rectangle: 12" x 5" x 5" (30.5 cm x 12.7 cm x 12.7cm)
• Triangle: 10" x 10" x 8½" (25.4 cm x 25.4 cm x 21.6 cm)
• Cone: 18" x 14" (45.7 cm x 33.6 cm)

MATERIALS

• 42" x 53" (111.8 cm x 157.5 cm) piece of iron-on fabric stabilizer, medium weight
• 12" x 19" (30.5 cm x 48.3 cm) piece of patterned cotton fabric (for ball)
• 20" x 29" (50.8 cm x 73.7 cm) piece of patterned cotton fabric (for cube)
• 12" x 29" (30.5 cm x 73.7 cm) piece of patterned cotton fabric (for triangle)
• 12" x 33" (30.5 cm x 83.8 cm) piece of patterned cotton fabric (for rectangle)
• 12" x 29" (30.5 cm x 73.7 cm) piece of patterned cotton fabric (for cone)
• Matching sewing thread
• Polyester fiberfill stuffing

TOOLS

• Chopstick
• Fabric pen
• Iron
• Pins
• Scissors
• Sewing machine
• Sewing needle

Figure A

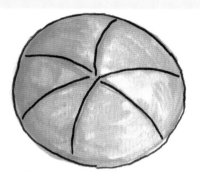

Figure B

Figure C

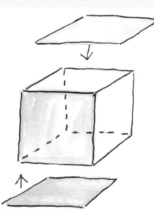

Figure D

Getting Started

• Copy Soft and Funky Building Shapes Pattern pieces (page 117), and cut.

• Iron fabric stabilizer onto backs of all fabric pieces.

• Trace Ball, Cube, Triangle, Triangle Bottom, Rectangle Bottom/Top, Rectangle Side, Cone, and Cone Bottom patterns onto fabric. Cut.

Instructions

Ball

STEP 1

Pin three ball pieces together, one beside the other, and sew seams.

STEP 2

Pin the other three ball pieces together, one beside the other, and sew seams (Figure A).

STEP 3

Pin first set of pieces to second set of pieces, right sides together. Sew along sides, and across top, bottom, and sides, leaving an opening for turning ball right side out.

STEP 4

Turn ball right side out. Insert stuffing, then slipstitch opening to close (Figure B).

Cube

STEP 1

Pin four cube pieces together, one beside the other (Figure C).

STEP 2

Sew seams along all four sides to make a closed shape.

STEP 3

Pin one cube piece on top and one cube piece on bottom. Make sure all right sides are facing inwards.

STEP 4

Sew top to sides. Sew bottom to sides, leaving an opening for turning cube right side out (Figure D). Make small slits in each corner.

STEP 5

Turn cube right side out. Insert stuffing, then slipstitch opening to close. Press sides to make a cube shape (Figure E).

Rectangle

STEP 1

Fold rectangle side piece (see pattern marking). Pin rectangle bottom/top pieces on top and bottom to make a closed shape. Make sure all right sides are facing inwards.

STEP 2

Sew sides to bottom and top, leaving an opening for turning right side out. Make small slits in each corner.

STEP 3

Turn rectangle right side out. Insert stuffing, then slipstitch opening to close. Press sides to make a rectangular shape (Figure F).

Triangle

STEP 1

Pin triangle side pieces together, one beside the other, and sew seams (Figure G).

STEP 2

Pin triangle bottom piece on bottom to make a closed shape (Figure H).

STEP 3

Sew along all three sides, leaving an opening for turning right side out. Make small slits in each corner.

STEP 4

Turn triangle right side out. Insert stuffing, then slipstitch opening to close (Figure I). Press sides to make a triangular shape.

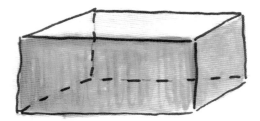

Figure F

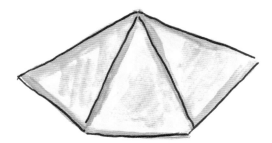

Figure G

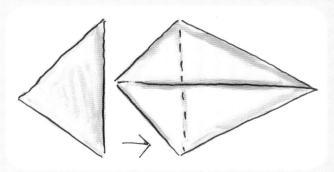

Figure H

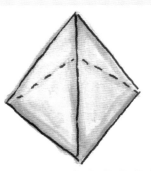

Figure I

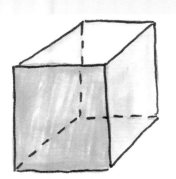

Figure E

51

Figure J

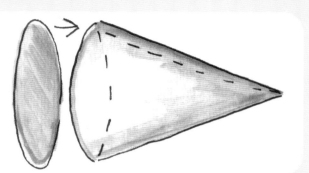

Figure K

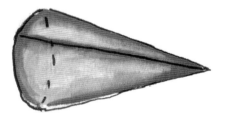

Figure L

Cone

STEP 1

Wrap cone piece around so that right and left ends meet, and pin. Sew a seam to make a closed shape (Figure J). Trim top of cone above stitching, so shape is pointy when turned right side out.

STEP 2

Pin cone bottom piece to cone base. Sew a seam all around base, leaving an opening for turning right side out (Figure K).

STEP 3

Turn right side out. Insert stuffing, then slipstitch opening to close. Press sides to make a cone shape (Figure L).

Striped Scalloped-Edged Blanket

No matter how many times you make this blanket it will always be unique thanks to the use of handmade striped fabric. I like using strips of fabric that have distinct personalities. For example, I like placing flowery designs alongside stripes, and polka dots beside checks. I also tend to vary the width of each strip for a more interesting look. Sometimes, the less something matches, the better!

EXPERIENCE LEVEL

DIMENSIONS

• 46" x 40" (116.8 cm x 101.6 cm)

MATERIALS

• Several strips of fabric, 46" (116.8 cm) long and 1" (2.6 cm) to 3" (7.6 cm) wide, in various colors and patterns (for striped fabric)

• 46" x 40" (116.8 cm x 101.6 cm) piece of cotton fabric (for lining)

• 46" x 40" (116.8 cm x 101.6 cm) piece of cotton batting (for filling)

• Matching sewing thread

• 164" (416.6 cm) piece of handmade bias tape

TOOLS

• Fabric pen
• Iron
• Pins

• Scissors
• Sewing machine
• Sewing needle

> For this blanket, I also used handmade bias tape to maximize its one-of-a-kind look.

Getting Started

• Copy Scalloped Edge Pattern (page 119), and cut.

• Trace Scalloped Edge pattern piece onto cotton batting and cotton lining, and cut.

Instructions

STEP 1

To make striped fabric, arrange strips of fabric vertically, one beside the other. Make sure fabrics with similar colors or patterns are not side by side.

STEP 2

Pin strips together to make a rectangular piece of fabric that is larger than 46" x 40" (116.8 cm x 101.6 cm).

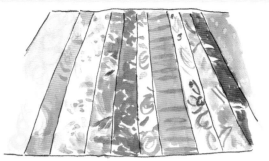

Figure A

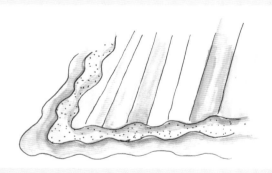

Figure B

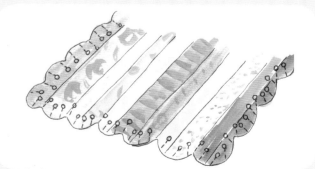

Figure C

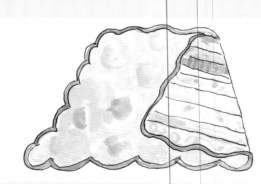

Figure D

STEP 3

Sew seams to connect strips, then press fabric on front. On the back, press with seams open (Figure A).

STEP 4

Trace Scalloped Edge Pattern onto wrong side of striped fabric, and cut (Figure B).

STEP 5

Lay cotton lining on your work surface, right side down. Lie batting on top, then lay striped fabric, right side up, on top of batting (Figure C).

STEP 6

Pin layers together all around (Figure D).

STEP 7

Sew a seam all around blanket, very close to the edge, to prepare blanket for bias tape (Figure E).

STEP 8

Pin bias tape all around, then sew (Figure F).

Figure E

Figure F

Baby's First Book

This book gives babies something visually stimulating to look at while they lie in their stroller or crib. I suggest using a variety of colorful fabrics for the pages. I chose fabrics with black, white, and red, since these are the first colors a baby's eyes can perceive. Both sides of every page should be different, so that you can turn the book over for a completely different look.

EXPERIENCE LEVEL

DIMENSIONS

- Folded: 6" x 6" (15.4 cm x 15.4 cm)
- Unfolded: 32" x 6" (81 cm x 15.4 cm)

MATERIALS

12 pieces of patterned cotton fabric, 7" x 7" (17.8 cm x 17.8 cm), in various colors and designs (such as stripes, polka dots, and plaids)

12" x 12" piece of satin fabric

21" x 28" (53.3 cm x 71.1 cm) piece of iron-on fabric stabilizer, medium weight

Matching thread (black, red, white)

17" x 13" (43.2 cm x 33.0 cm) piece of foam, ¼" thick

TOOLS

- Fabric pen
- Iron
- Pins
- Scissors
- Sewing machine
- Sewing needle

When your baby outgrows this book, it makes a beautiful wall hanging. Simply unfold the book and hang it on the wall. Since both sides are different, it can be flipped over every now and again for a change in scenery.

Getting Started

- Copy Baby's First Book Pattern pieces (page 119), and cut.
- Iron fabric stabilizer onto backs of all fabric pieces.
- Trace Inside Page, Last Page, and Cover patterns onto fabric, and cut.
- Trace Shapes for Appliqué pattern onto satin, and cut.
- Trace Foam pattern onto foam, and cut.

Figure A

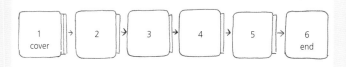

Figure B

Figure C

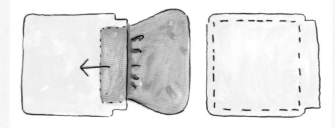

Figure D

Instructions

STEP 1

Pin appliqué pieces onto inside pages, cover, or last page, any combination you like. Zigzag around each appliqué with matching thread (Figure A).

STEP 2

Pin pairs of page pieces, right sides together, making sure front and back of each page is different.

STEP 3

Arrange pages in any order you like, but following tab order (Figure B).

STEP 4

Cover: Pin pair of cover pieces, wrong sides together. Sew around 3 sides, leaving tab area open for turning right side out and inserting foam (Figure C).

STEP 5

Turn cover right side out, and press. Insert a piece of foam, press, and overstitch on 4 sides (Figure D).

STEP 6

Pages: Pin pairs of page pieces, wrong sides together. Sew around 3 sides of each page, starting at top notch, and sewing around until bottom notch. Leave opening for turning page right side out and inserting foam (Figure E).

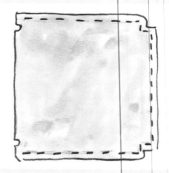

Figure E

STEP 7

Turn under opening of each page for a clean finish, and press (Figure F).

STEP 8

Turn page right side out, press, and insert foam (Figure G).

STEP 9

Insert cover tab into opening of first page, and pin (Figure H).

STEP 10

Overstitch around first page to connect it to cover. Make sure overstitch catches cover tab as you sew around page (Figure I).

STEP 11

Continue to insert page tabs into adjacent pages, overstitching each new page to connect it (Figure J).

STEP 12

Add page without tab last.

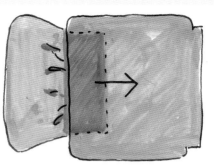

Figure G

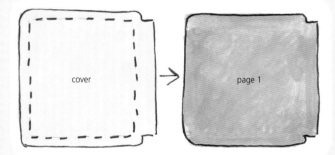

Figure H

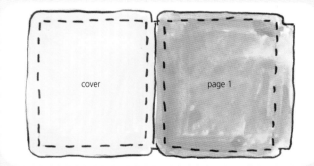

Figure I

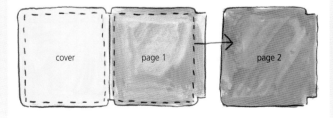

Figure J

Figure F

Awake/Asleep Elephant Sachet

This adorable stuffed animal has a subtle way of letting people know whether baby is sleeping or not. I've selected an elephant for this design, but you can use any animal you like (flip through the Project Patterns on pages 108-128 for other ideas).

EXPERIENCE LEVEL

DIMENSIONS

- 9" x 9½" (22.9 cm x 24.2 cm)

MATERIALS

- 10" x 25" (25.4 cm x 63.5 cm) gray wool fabric
- 4" x 6" (10.2 cm x 15.2 cm) piece of white lace
- 4" x 4" (10.2 cm x 10.2 cm) piece of red wool fabric
- Matching sewing thread (gray, white)
- 1 doll eye
- Black and pink embroidery thread (for eyes and mouth)
- Polyester fiberfill stuffing
- 8" (20.3 cm) piece of yellow ribbon

TOOLS

- Chopstick
- Embroidery needle
- Fabric pen
- Iron
- Pins
- Scissors
- Sewing machine
- Sewing needle

To make a scented sachet, replace some of the fiberfill stuffing with dry lavender. The sachet can then be placed in a dresser drawer or closet to provide a lovely, delicate scent.

Figure A

Figure B

Figure C

Figure D

Getting Started

• Copy Awake/Asleep Elephant Sachet Pattern pieces, and cut.

• Trace Elephant, Ear and Eyelid patterns onto gray fabric, and cut.

• Cut lace into two pieces: one 4" x 4" (10.2 cm x 10.2 cm) and one 2" x 2" (5.1 cm x 5.1 cm).

Instructions

STEP 1

Blanket stitch around the rounded part of each ear piece, from top tab to bottom tab, leaving tab area unsewn (Figure A).

STEP 2

Cut slits on elephant pieces (see pattern marking). Insert an ear tab inside each slit, so that rounded part of ear faces front of elephant (Figure B).

STEP 3

Fold front of elephant piece backwards over ear, and sew a seam across ear tab, where it pokes through body (Figure C).

STEP 4

Sew a blanket stitch around rounded part of eyelid piece. Make eyelashes by embroidering several backstitches (Figure D).

STEP 5

Embroider sleeping eye on one elephant piece, and sew doll eye onto other elephant piece. Embroider mouth with satin stitch.

STEP 6

Fold ribbon into a loop. Pin loop onto top of one elephant piece, with loop facing downward. Sew down (Figure E).

STEP 7

Pin elephant pieces, right sides together. Sew a seam all around, sewing down top of ribbon loop as well. Leave an opening at the bottom for turning right side out.

STEP 8

Turn elephant right side out. Insert stuffing, then slipstitch opening to close. Steam (Figure F).

STEP 9

Sew larger lace square onto red wool square by zigzagging around edges and making a straight stitch in the center. Hand-sew large and small lace pieces onto elephant (Figures G and H).

Figure E

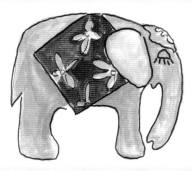

Figure F

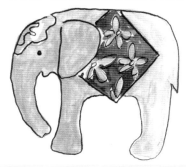

Figure G

Figure H

63

Count-the-Sheep-to-Sleep Mobile

This mobile consists of four fluffy sheep, but you can make it with any stuffed animal that you like (or with several different animals). When hanging the mobile, make sure it is high enough above the crib so that baby can't reach it. I like hanging a mobile over the changing table, since I find the mobile keeps baby busy (thereby reducing wiggling!) while I change the diaper.

EXPERIENCE LEVEL

DIMENSIONS
• 28½" x 8" (72.4 cm x 20.3 cm)
• 18" (45.7 cm) from top of tent to bottom of sheep

MATERIALS
Mobile
• 14" x 18" (35.6 cm x 45.7 cm) piece of cotton fabric (for top)
• 14" x 18" (35.6 cm x 45.7 cm) piece of cotton fabric (for lining)
• Matching sewing thread (white)
• 20" (51 cm) piece of white ribbon (for hanging mobile)
• 36" (91.4 cm) piece of white bias tape
• 36" (91.4 cm) piece of plastic boning, ⅛" (0.3 cm) wide
• 36" (91.4 cm) piece of ball fringe

Sheep
• 8" x 4" (20.3 cm x 10.2 cm) piece of black felt (for ears, muzzles, and legs)
• 4 handfuls of Bergshaft or Shetland wool (for sheep bodies and heads)
• Unprocessed curly white wool (for sheep bodies, optional)
• Matching sewing thread (black)
• Plastic fishing line or strong white thread (for hanging the sheep)
• Mobile arm, with or without music (for hanging the mobile, optional)

TOOLS
• Fabric pen
• Felting needle (medium) or needle holder that holds 3 needles at once
• Long doll needle
• Pins
• Scissors
• Sewing machine
• Foam square (for felting)

A few words about wool
The sheep in this mobile are made from raw wool that is felted with a needle. I recommend using rough wool such as Shetland or Bergshaft. You can buy it at craft stores, online, or at a sheep farm. In addition to the wool that is felted, I added an outer layer of unprocessed wool that I bought, freshly sheared, at the Indiana State Fair. The unprocessed wool is curly and gives the little sheep a more realistic look.

About felting
Felting is a time-consuming process, but the results are wonderful! Remember to keep the felting needle straight as it goes up and down into the wool; otherwise, it will break. Always work on a piece of foam, take your time, and be very careful!

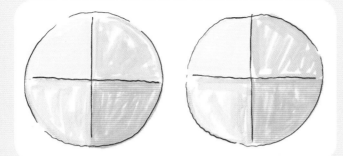

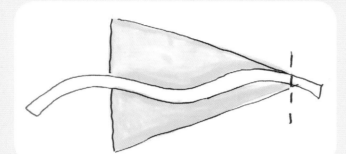

Figure A

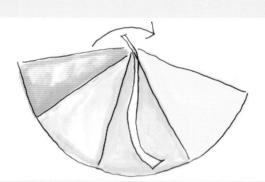

Figure B

Figure C

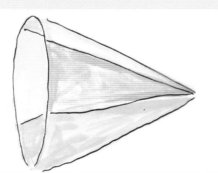

Figure D

Getting Started

• Trace Count-the-Sheep-to-Sleep Mobile Pattern pieces (page 121), and cut.

• Trace Mobile pattern onto cotton fabric, and cut (Figure A).
Note: The top is what you see; the lining is what baby sees.

• Trace Ear, Leg, and Muzzle patterns onto black felt, and cut.

Instructions

Mobile tent

STEP 1

To make mobile top: Sew ribbon onto tip of one top mobile piece (Figure B).

STEP 2

Pin this top piece to three other top mobile pieces, one after the other, to make a cone shape. (The ribbon should extend from the top of the cone.) Sew pieces together (Figures C and D).

STEP 3

To make mobile lining: Pin mobile lining pieces together, one after the other, to make a cone shape. Sew pieces together.

STEP 4

Stack cones on each other, wrong sides together. Hand-stitch cone points together (Figure E).

STEP 5

Straight stitch around base of mobile (Figure F).

STEP 6

Pin bias tape around outer edge of mobile base. Fold bias tape inside mobile to form a tunnel, and sew all around mobile base. Leave bias tape ends open.

STEP 7

Slide plastic boning inside bias tape tunnel. Plastic should be a little longer than the mobile base circumference, so that it overlaps inside the tunnel (Figure G).

STEP 8

Sew ball fringe around outside of mobile, along base.

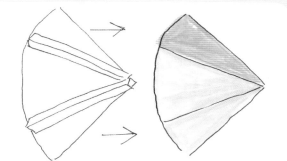

Figure E

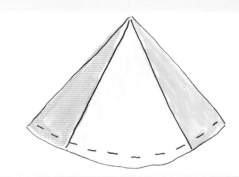

Figure F

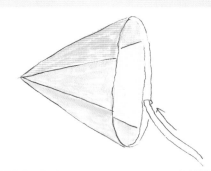

Figure G

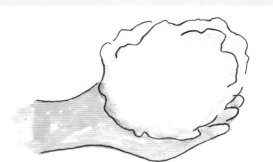

Figure H

Figure I

Figure J

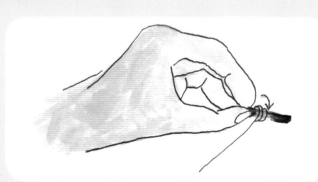

Figure K

Sheep

STEP 1

For each sheep body, grasp a handful of wool, and wad it up into a ball. With felting needle, poke wool all around until a firm oval shape forms. If ball is too small, add another layer of wool, and poke again until firm. Your finished piece should have a circumference of about 6" (15.2 cm) (Figures H and I).

STEP 2

For each sheep head, grasp a smaller bunch of wool, and wad it up into a ball. Felt the ball as you did for the body, until it has a circumference of about 1½" (3.8 cm).

STEP 3

To make each muzzle, roll muzzle piece into a cylinder. Felt with one felting needle until an oval shape forms. Place muzzle on head, then felt all around, poking needle around muzzle base to secure onto head.

STEP 4

Place head on body, and use one felting needle to felt around head, poking it onto body. Make sure you poke head onto ball exterior, not through ball. If you like, add curly wool to body and head by poking it gently into the wool balls, using the felting needle (Figure J).

STEP 5

Poke ear pieces into head with felting needle.

STEP 6

Roll each leg piece into a cylinder. Make a stitch at cylinder top with black embroidery thread, then wrap thread several times around entire length of leg (Figure K). Make another stitch at the bottom.

STEP 7

Cut two horizontal slits across bottom of sheep belly, deep enough for inserting the legs (Figure L). Insert all four legs evenly into slits. With a single felting needle, felt small pieces of white wool into slits around sheep's legs, to close slits. If you like, add more curly pieces of wool around legs and belly, to make the sheep woollier (Figure M).

STEP 8

Thread long doll needle with plastic fishing line, and tie a knot at one end. Draw fishing line up through the belly of each sheep, and into lining of mobile. Draw thread through lining and tie a secure knot. Tie ribbon at top of mobile to a hook screwed into the ceiling, or to a mobile arm (Figure N).

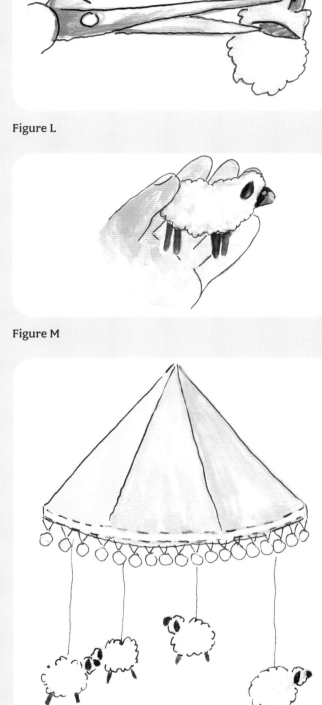

Figure L

Figure M

Figure N

 Bird-in-Nest

This beautiful little bird and nest make a pretty adornment for any child's room. You can make one bird or a whole flock of them, in a variety of colors and patterns. Each bird features several loops of ribbon that are great for keeping curious young minds and fingers busy. Make the loops in various sizes and colors.

EXPERIENCE LEVEL

DIMENSIONS

- Bird: 9" x 5½" x 3½" (22.9 cm x 14 cm x 8.9 cm)
- Nest: 13" x 3½" (33 cm x 8.9 cm)

MATERIALS
Bird

- 9" x 10" (22.9 cm x 25.4 cm) piece of blue and white (or desired color) cotton gingham fabric (for each bird)
- 25" (63.5 cm) piece of blue satin ribbon (for wings and tail)
- 3" (7.6 cm) piece of yellow satin ribbon (for beak)
- Matching sewing thread (blue)
- Light blue embroidery thread (for eyes)
- Polyester fiberfill stuffing

Nest

- 10" x 10" (25.4 cm x 25.4cm) piece of light brown and white cotton gingham (for nest)
- 10" x 10" (25.4 cm x 25.4cm) piece of dark brown cotton (for lining)
- 10" x 10" (25.4 cm x 25.4cm) piece of polyester fiberfill batting
- Matching sewing thread (brown)

TOOLS

- Embroidery needle
- Fabric pen
- Iron
- Pins
- Scissors
- Sewing machine
- Sewing needle
- Sleeve board

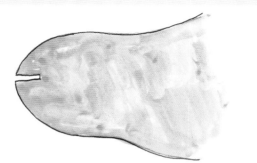

Figure A

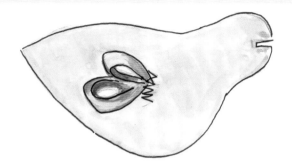

Figure B

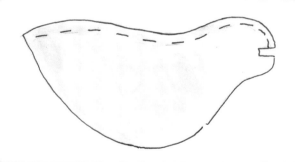

Figure C

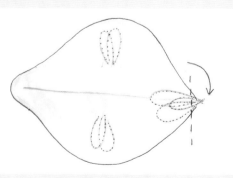

Figure D

Getting Started

• Bird: Copy Bird-in-Nest Pattern pieces (page 122), and cut.

• Trace Bird Side and Bird Bottom patterns, and cut. Be sure to cut a slit for the beak, as pattern indicates (Figure A).

• Nest: Trace Nest pattern onto light brown gingham, dark brown cotton, and batting. Cut.

Instructions

Bird

STEP 1

To make each wing, fold an 8" (20.3 cm) piece of blue ribbon into 2 loops. Zigzag loops onto each bird side piece (see pattern marking) (Figure B).

STEP 2

Pin bird side pieces, wrong sides together. Sew a seam along top (Figure C).

STEP 3

Spread bird sides open so that they lie flat on your work surface, with right sides facing upwards (Figure D).

STEP 4

To make tail, fold a 9" (22.9 cm) piece of blue ribbon into 3 loops (Figure E).

STEP 5

Make a stitch across all three loops to secure, then pin at back end of bird, with loops pointing toward head. Sew across loops to secure in place.

STEP 6

To make beak, fold yellow ribbon into 2 loops. Make a stitch across both loops to secure (Figure F).

STEP 7

Place bird sides, right sides together. Lift top bird side, and insert beak loops into slit in head of bottom bird side, with loops facing the tail. Make a small stitch to secure beak loops. Place upper bird side down, making sure tail and beak ribbons are sandwiched between bird sides, and are not in the area where seams will be sewn. (Figures G and H).

STEP 8

Sew all around bird body. Sew reinforcing stitches on each side of beak.

STEP 9

Embroider a French knot on each side, for eyes (Figure I).

STEP 10

With wrong sides together, pin bird bottom piece along bottom of side pieces. Sew a seam all around, leaving an opening for turning bird right side out (Figure J).

STEP 11

Turn bird right side out. Insert stuffing, then slipstitch opening to close.

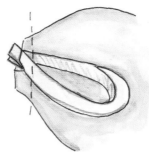

Figure G

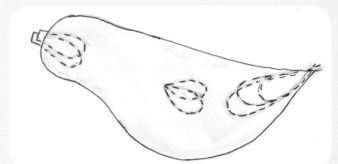

Figure H

Figure I

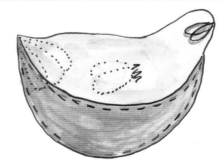

Figure J

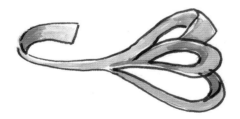

Figure E

Figure F

Figure K

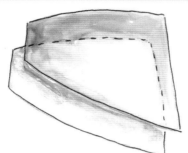

Figure L

Figure M

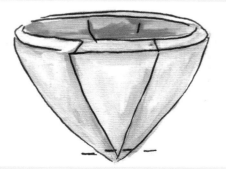

Figure N

Nest

STEP 1

Pin gingham nest pieces together, one beside the other. Sew seams to make a bowl (Figure K). Straight stitch along bottom of bowl to ensure pieces are connected and that there are no spaces.

STEP 2

Pin batting nest pieces to wrong side of dark brown nest pieces. Sew a seam all around each piece (Figures L and M).

STEP 3

Pin dark brown-batting nest pieces together, one beside the other. Sew seams to make a bowl. Straight stitch along bottom of bowl to ensure nest pieces are connected and that there are no spaces (Figure N).

STEP 4

Place bowls one inside the other, with right sides facing, so that batting side of one bowl and raw side of other bowl are facing out. Pin bowls together. Sew a seam around edge, leaving an opening for turning right side out (Figure O).

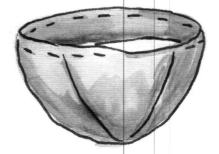

Figure O

STEP 5

Turn nest right side out. It should now look like a ball, with batting on the inside (Figure P).

STEP 6

Push down top of ball shape, pressing it into bottom of ball shape, to make a bowl shape again (Figure Q). Slipstitch opening to close.

STEP 7

Quilt a circular pattern around nest (Figure R). Press into shape.

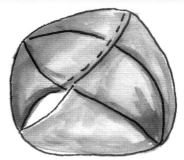

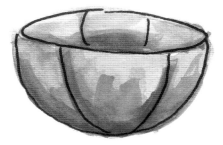

Figure P

Figure Q

Figure R

 Family Photo Cube

In my family, we often strove to make items that had more than one function. In this project, a square toy is also a photograph album and room decoration. Use photographs with familiar faces, such as Grandma and Grandpa, aunts and uncles, cousins and friends, or family pets. Switch the photographs as often as you like.

EXPERIENCE LEVEL

DIMENSIONS

• 9½" x 9½" x 9½" (24.2 cm x 24.2 cm x 24.2 cm)

MATERIALS

• Six 10" x 10" (25.4 cm x 25.4 cm) pieces of patterned cotton fabric, diverse matching patterns

• 30" x 30" (76.2 cm x 76.2 cm) piece of iron-on fabric stabilizer, medium weight

• 28" x 19" (71.1 cm x 48.3 cm) pieces of foam, ¼" (0.6 cm) thick

• 10" x 21" (25.4 cm x 53.3 cm) piece of clear vinyl

• Thick sewing thread (for sewing vinyl)

• Polyester fiberfill stuffing

TOOLS

• Embroidery needle

• Fabric pen or tailor's chalk

• Iron

• Pins

• Pressing cloth (for pressing vinyl)

• Scissors

• Sewing machine with presser foot made for vinyl

• Sewing needle

Figure A

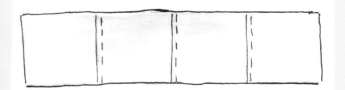

Figure B

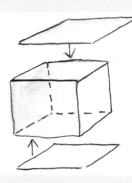

Figure C

Getting Started

- Trace Family Photo Cube Pattern (page 123), and cut.
- Use a scissor blade to mark holes corresponding to dots on Photo Cube pattern.
- Iron fabric stabilizer onto backs of cotton fabric pieces. Trace Photo Cube pattern onto cotton, and cut. Mark holes in pattern onto fabric pieces.
- Trace Foam pattern onto foam, and cut.
- Trace Window pattern onto vinyl, and cut.

Instructions

STEP 1

Set sewing machine for sewing vinyl. Pin a window piece in the center of each photo cube piece (see pattern marking). Using a plastic presser foot and thick sewing thread, sew three sides of each window, leaving the top open. Make sure you sew the same three sides of each vinyl piece (Figure A).

STEP 2

Pin four photo cube pieces together, one beside the other (Figure B) to make a closed shape. Make sure all window openings are oriented in the same direction. Sew seams along all four sides.

STEP 3

Pin one photo cube piece on top and one photo cube piece on bottom, to make a cube shape. Make sure all right sides are facing inwards.

STEP 4

Sew top to sides, then sew bottom to sides, leaving an opening for turning cube right side out (Figure C). Make small slits in each corner.

STEP 5

Pin foam pieces together, in same way that fabric pieces were pinned, to make a cube. Sew seams on all sides, leaving an opening for turning cube right side out.

STEP 6

Turn foam cube right side out. Turn fabric cube right side out. Insert foam cube into fabric cube, making sure corners and openings are lined up (Figures D and E).

STEP 7

Insert stuffing into foam cube until cube is firm, but not overstuffed. (You want the sides to be flat, not rounded.) Slipstitch opening in foam cube, then fabric cube, to close. Using a pressing cloth, steam sides to make a cube shape (Figure F).

STEP 8

To insert photos into windows, push down fabric inside the window with one hand, and slide photo in with the other hand. Remove photos using same technique (Figure G).

Figure D

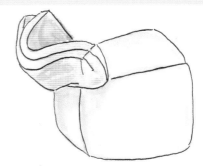

Figure E

Figure F

Figure G

Bunny-Carrot-Bunny Flag

This flag is a fun, easy-to-make room decoration. You can use the same shapes several times, or use a variety of shapes. For example, to make a farm flag, make stuffed ponies, roosters, and cats. To make a jungle flag, make lions, elephants and giraffes.

EXPERIENCE LEVEL

DIMENSIONS

• Each bunny: 7" x 9" (17.8 cm x 22.9 cm)
• Each carrot: 2" x 5" (5.1 cm x 12.7 cm)
• Entire flag: 80" x 7" (203.1 cm x 17.8 cm)

MATERIALS

• 3" x 3½" (7.6 cm x 8.9 cm) piece of pink felt (for bunny ears)
• 31" x 33" (78.7 cm x 83.8 cm) piece of cream wool fabric (for bunny bodies)
• 12" x 16" (30.5 cm x 40.6 cm) piece of orange felt (for carrots)
• 5½" x 8" (14 cm x 20.3 cm) piece of green felt (for carrot tops)
• Matching thread (pink, white, green, orange)
• Polyester fiberfill stuffing
• 6" (15.2 cm) piece of marabou
• White and black embroidery thread (for legs and eyes)
• 80" (203.1 cm) piece of cotton rope, ¼" (0.6 cm) wide

TOOLS

• Chopstick
• Embroidery needle
• Fabric pen
• Iron
• Pins
• Scissors
• Sewing machine
• Sewing needle

You can also use this pattern to make a scented sachet. Simply stuff the bunny with a bit of dry lavender before closing. To make a bunny pillow, increase the pattern by 300%.

Be sure to hang flags high enough so that even if baby stands on a crib toy or two, the flags will be well out of reach.

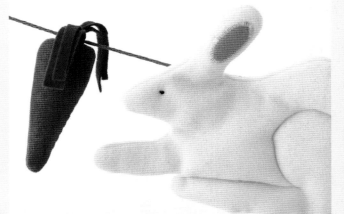

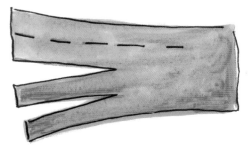

Figure A

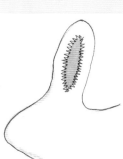

Figure B

Figure C

Figure D

Getting Started

- Copy Bunny-Carrot-Bunny Flag pattern pieces (page 124), and cut.
- Fold pink felt in half, and pin. Trace Inner Ear pattern, and cut.
- Fold cream wool in half, and pin. Trace Bunny pattern, and cut.
- Fold orange felt in half, and pin. Trace Carrot pattern, and cut.
- Fold green felt in half, and pin. Trace Carrot Top pattern, and cut (Figure A).
- Make three short vertical cuts in Carrot Top (see pattern marking) to make fringe.

Instructions

To make this bunny flag, you'll need to make six bunnies and six carrots.

Bunny

STEP 1

Pin an inner ear piece on 6 bunny pieces (see pattern marking). Zigzag around inner ear pieces with matching thread (Figure B).

STEP 2

Pin pairs of bunny pieces, right sides together, so that one bunny in each pair has an ear. Sew a seam all around, leaving an opening near the tail for turning right side out (Figure C).

STEP 3

Turn bunny right side out and insert stuffing. Don't insert too much stuffing because you want the bunny to be puffy, yet flat. Slipstitch opening to close. Press.

STEP 4

With matching thread, embroider a running stitch to define the hind legs. For the tail, sew on a piece of marabou (Figure D). Embroider eyes with French knots and a mouth with backstitch.

Carrot

STEP 1

Roll up uncut short end of one carrot top piece. Sew across rolled area to keep it from unrolling (Figure E).

Figure E

STEP 2

Pin rolled end of carrot top piece to wrong side of one carrot piece, along thicker end, so that fringes on carrot top piece face thinner end of carrot.

STEP 3

Place another carrot piece on top, wrong side facing, so that carrot top piece is sandwiched between carrot pieces. Pin. Sew a seam all around, leaving a small opening for turning carrot right side out. (Figure F).

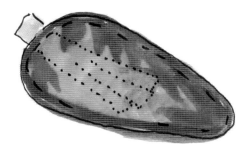

Figure F

STEP 4

Turn carrot right side out, and insert fiberfill stuffing. Slipstitch opening to close. Press.

Flag

STEP 1

Pin bunnies and carrots to cotton rope in an alternating pattern, at even intervals of about 2" (5.1 cm) (Figure G).

Figure G

STEP 2

Hand-sew bunnies and carrots onto rope. Sew bunnies at two places (Figure H) to secure them firmly.

Figure H

🐻 Baby Bear Bib 🐻

I made a variety of bibs for my girls when they were little. This design was one of my (and their!) favorites. In addition to being adorable, it's also quite practical, since the big bear face protects the entire front of baby's body, catching almost anything that falls or dribbles. The bib is made with terry cloth and cotton, making it thick, absorbent, and easy to wash.

EXPERIENCE LEVEL

DIMENSIONS

• 15" x 17" (38.1 cm x 43.2 cm)

MATERIALS

• 18" x 20" (45.7 cm x 50.8 cm) piece of beige terry cloth (for front)

• 17" x 18" (43.2 cm x 45.7 cm) piece of beige cotton fabric (for back)

• 9" x 7" (22.9 cm x 17.8 cm) piece of white cotton fabric (for muzzle and inner ear)

• 3" x 3" (7.6 cm x 7.6 cm) piece of black cotton fabric (for nose)

• 9" x 10" (22.9 cm x 25.4 cm) piece of iron-on fabric stabilizer, medium weight

• Matching sewing thread (beige, white, black)

• Black and red embroidery thread (for eyes and mouth)

• 66" (167.5 cm) piece of bias tape (optional)

• 2" x 2" (5.1 cm x 5.1 cm) piece of Velcro®

TOOLS

• Embroidery needle
• Fabric Pen
• Iron
• Pins
• Scissors
• Sewing machine
• Sewing needle

Figure A

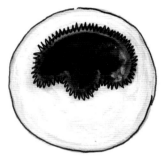

Figure B

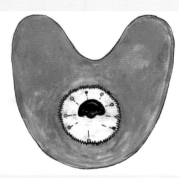

Figure C

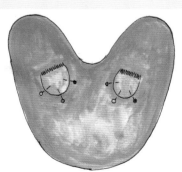

Figure D

Getting Started

• Copy Bear Bib Pattern pieces (page 125), and cut.

• Pin terry cloth and cotton fabric with wrong sides together. Trace Bib and Outer Ear patterns, and cut.

• Iron fabric stabilizer onto back of white and black cotton. Trace Nose pattern onto black fabric, and cut. Trace Muzzle and Inner Ear patterns onto white fabric, and cut.

Instructions

STEP 1

Pin inner ear pieces onto outer ear pieces (see pattern marking). Zigzag all around inner ear with matching thread (Figure A).

STEP 2

Pin pairs of outer ear pieces, right sides together, so that one side of each pair has an inner ear. Sew a seam all around, leaving an opening at the bottom for turning ears right side out. Turn ears right side out. Press.

STEP 3

Pin nose piece onto muzzle piece (see pattern marking). Zigzag all around nose with matching thread (Figure B).

STEP 4

Pin muzzle onto terry cloth bib piece (see pattern marking). Zigzag all around muzzle with matching thread (Figure C).

STEP 5

Place ears on bib piece, face down and at an angle (see pattern marking). Zigzag along straight line (Figure D).

STEP 6

Fold ears up, then straight stitch in a straight line along bottom of each ear (Figure E).

STEP 7

Embroider eyes with French knots, and a mouth with backstitch.

STEP 8

Pin bib front and back, with wrong sides together. Sew a seam all around, close to the edge, to prepare for bias tape (Figure F).

STEP 9

Pin bias tape all around and sew (Figure G).

STEP 10

Sew stiff half of Velcro® onto front of bib, on one side. Sew soft half of Velcro® onto back of bib, on other side (Figure H).

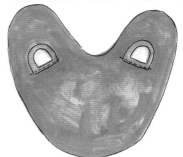

Figure E

Figure F

Figure G

Figure H

 Striped Baby Bib

I find bibs are especially useful when baby is wearing his or her best clothes. Of course, if your baby is wearing something special, you don't want to cover it up with a really big bib. That's why this small dribble bib is so handy: it's big enough to protect your baby's clothes, but not so big that it covers up a favorite outfit. This project is so easy, you can make several bibs, to match several outfits.

EXPERIENCE LEVEL

DIMENSIONS

• 10" x 9½" (25.4 cm x 24.2 cm)

MATERIALS

• 10" x 10" (25.4 cm x 25.4 cm) piece of handmade striped fabric (pages 53-54) (for front)
• 10" x 10" (25.4 cm x 25.4 cm) piece of cotton (for lining)
• Matching sewing thread
• 55" (139.7 cm) piece of bias tape

TOOLS

• Fabric pen
• Pins
• Scissors
• Sewing machine

Antique tablecloths, pillowcases, and decorative doilies often sold at flea markets and garage sales are excellent sources of decorative fabric. Even if the fabric isn't in perfect condition, you can simply cut out and use the parts that look nice.

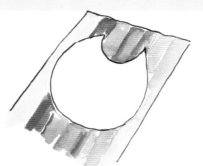

Figure A

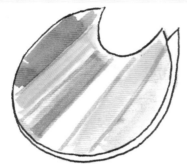

Figure B

Figure C

Figure D

Getting Started

• Copy Striped Baby Bib Pattern (page 126), and cut.

• Place cotton and striped fabric together, and pin.

• Trace Bib pattern, and cut (Figures A and B).

> Reduce the Striped Baby Bib pattern by 50% and you'll have a terrific doll bib.

Instructions

STEP 1

Pin striped and cotton bib pieces, wrong sides together. Sew a seam all around, close to the edge, to prepare for sewing on bias tape (Figure C).

STEP 2

Pin bias tape around outer edge, and sew (Figure D).

STEP 3

Pin bias tape around neck area, leaving 10" (25.4 cm) tails on either side, and sew (Figure E).

STEP 4

Fold under bias tape ends at both ends, making two ½" (1.3 cm) hems on each side, for a clean edge. Press and sew (Figure F).

STEP 5

Fold each bias tape tie lengthwise in half. Press and sew (Figure G).

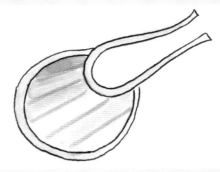

Figure E

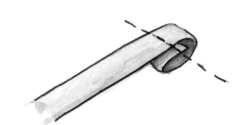

Figure F

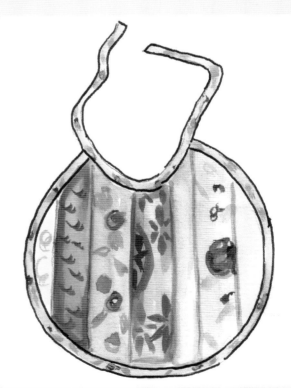

Figure G

 Adorable Elf Slippers

These slippers were originally part of an elf costume; one of the most popular costumes in my children's boutique. The slippers are so cute and comfortable that many kids wear them long after they've taken off their costume. They are great for keeping toes and ankles toasty warm all year long.

EXPERIENCE LEVEL

DIMENSIONS

- Size: 12 months
- Sole: 2 " x 5 " (5.1 cm x 12.7 cm)
- Height: 4 " (10.2 cm)

MATERIALS

- 17 " x 24 " (43.2 cm x 61 cm) piece of green fleece (for slippers)
- 7 " x 7 " (17.8 cm x 17.8 cm) piece of thin foam or cotton batting (for soles)
- 7 " x 7 " (17.8 cm x 17.8 cm) piece of textured vinyl (for soles)
- 7 " x 7 " (17.8 cm x 17.8 cm) piece of cotton fabric (for soles)
- Matching sewing thread (green)
- Polyester fiberfill stuffing

TOOLS

- Chopstick
- Fabric pen
- Pins
- Iron
- Scissors
- Sewing machine
- Sewing needle

Getting Started

- Copy Adorable Elf Slippers Pattern pieces (page 127), and cut.
- Fold green fleece in half, and pin. With fleece fibers running horizontally, lay Slipper and Lining patterns on fleece, and trace. Cut.
- Trace Sole pattern onto foam, vinyl, and cotton fabric, and cut.

Instructions

Slipper

STEP 1

Set sewing machine for sewing stretchy fabrics. Pin a pair of lining pieces, right sides together. Sew at bottom only, up to notch (Figure A).

Figure A

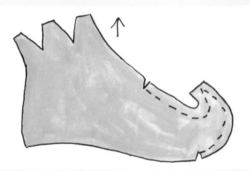

Figure B

Figure C

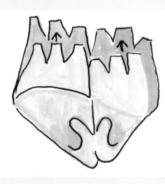

Figure D

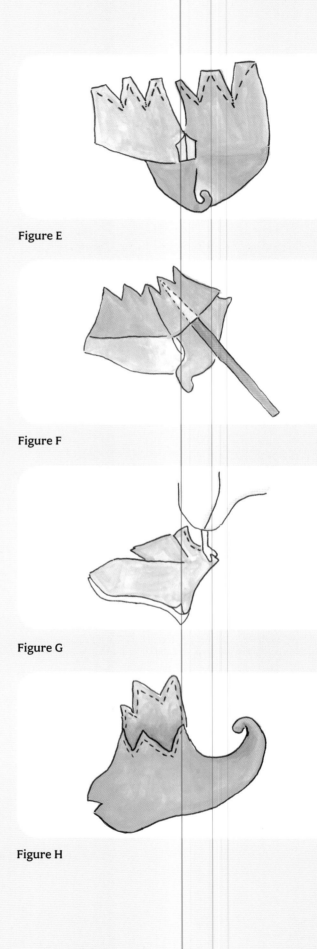

Figure E

Figure F

Figure G

Figure H

STEP 2

Pin a pair of slipper pieces, right sides together. Sew a seam around toe area, from notch to notch (Figure B).

STEP 3

Turn slipper right side out. Use a chopstick to push out curly tip (Figure C).

STEP 4

Pin lining pieces to slipper pieces, right sides together. Sew a seam along top cuff points. Cut slits in corners, and trim points (Figures D and E).

STEP 5

Turn slipper cuff right side out. Use a chopstick to push out points (Figure F).

STEP 6

With right sides together, sew together lining heel and slipper heel (Figure G). Trim corners. Overstitch along tops of points (Figure H).

Sole

STEP 1

Set sewing machine for sewing ordinary fabrics. Sandwich foam sole piece between vinyl and cotton sole pieces, so that wrong sides of vinyl and sole face foam (Figure I). Pin, then sew a seam all around (Figure J).

STEP 2

Match notches on sole and slipper, and pin right sides together (Figure K). Tuck curly tip of slipper inside, then sew a seam all around sole (Figure L).

STEP 3

Turn slipper right side out, and press. Using a chopstick, insert a little polyester fiberfill into curly tip.

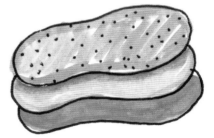

Figure I

Figure J

Figure K

Figure L

Puppy Sunhat

Some babies don't like wearing sunhats, so having one that's really cute can make all the difference!
I recommend using natural fibers that stay cool in the summer heat. If your baby loves pulling off the hat,
attach ribbons on either side for tying under the chin.

EXPERIENCE LEVEL

DIMENSIONS

• Size: 12 months
• 20" (50.8 cm) circumference

MATERIALS

• 14" x 34" (35.6 cm x 86.4 cm) piece of thick beige cotton fabric (for hat and ears)
• 14" x 34" (35.6 cm x 86.4 cm) piece of iron-on fabric stabilizer, medium weight
• 4" x 4" (10.2 cm x 10.2 cm) piece of white cotton fabric (for muzzle)
• 2" x 2" (5.1 cm x 5.1 cm) piece of black cotton fabric (for nose)
• 5" x 6" (12.7 cm x 15.2 cm) piece of beige and white cotton gingham fabric (for ear lining)
• Matching sewing thread (beige, black, white)
• Black and red embroidery thread (for eyes, mouth, and tongue)
• Embroidery needle
• 21" (53.3 cm) piece of red and white checked piping
• 16" (40.6 cm) thin ribbon (optional, for ties)

TOOLS

• Fabric pen
• Iron
• Scissors
• Sewing machine with zipper foot
• Sewing needle
• Sleeve board

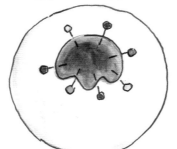

Figure A

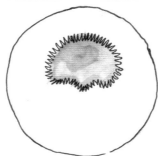

Figure B

Figure C

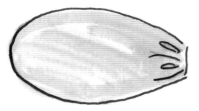

Figure D

Getting Started

For this project, mark patterns on beige cotton first, then iron fabric stabilizer on back of pattern pieces that need it. After that, cut all the pieces at the same time.

• Copy Puppy Sunhat Pattern pieces (page 128), and cut.

• Trace Hat, Ear, Front Brim, and Back Brim patterns onto beige cotton.

• Iron fabric stabilizer on back of Front and Back Brim patterns. Cut out patterns.

• Iron fabric stabilizer onto white and black cotton fabrics. Trace Muzzle pattern onto white fabric, and cut. Trace Nose pattern onto black cotton, and cut.

• Trace Ear pattern onto gingham, and cut.

Instructions

STEP 1

Pin nose piece onto muzzle piece (see pattern marking) (Figure A). Zigzag around nose with matching thread (Figure B).

STEP 2

Pin muzzle piece onto one hat piece (see pattern marking). Zigzag around muzzle with matching thread.

STEP 3

Embroider eyes with French knots, a mouth with backstitch, and a tongue with satin stitch (Figure C).

STEP 4

Pin each beige ear piece to a gingham ear piece, right sides together. Sew a seam all around, leaving an opening along straight side for turning ear right side out, and making gathers.

STEP 5

Turn ears right side out, and make gathers along straight edge (Figure D).

STEP 6

Align gathered side of ears with upper edges of hat piece with face, so that gingham is face down, and ears cover eyes (Figure E). Stitch down ears (Figure F).

STEP 7

Pin one hat piece on either side of hat piece with face, to make front of hat. Zigzag raw edges on underside. Make sure tops of ears are sewn in at the same time.

STEP 8

To make back of hat, pin three hat pieces together, one beside the other. Zigzag seams on underside (Figure G).

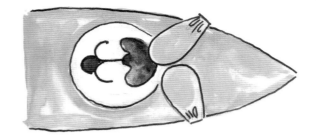

Figure E

Figure F

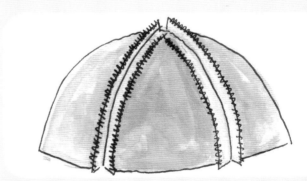

Figure G

Figure H

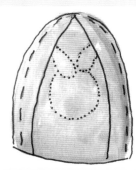

Figure I

Figure J

Figure K

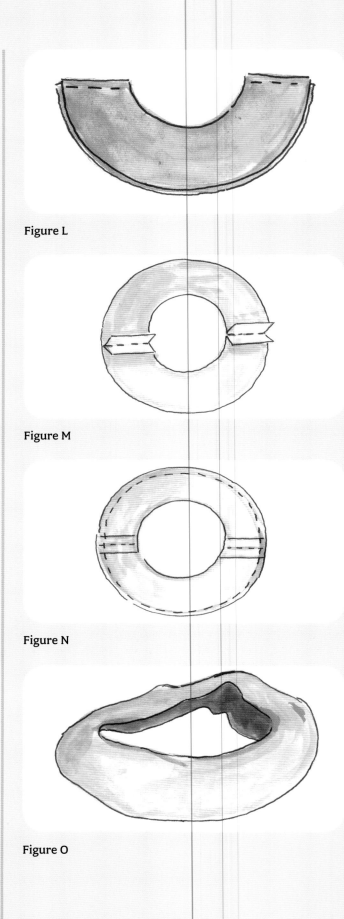

Figure L

Figure M

Figure N

Figure O

STEP 9

Pin front of hat to back of hat, right sides together. Sew a ½"
(1.3 cm) seam to connect the two pieces, leaving bottom open.
Zigzag the edges (Figures H and I).

STEP 10

Sew piping around base of hat (Figures J and K).

STEP 11

Pin each brim front piece to a brim back piece, and sew along straight
edges (Figure L).

STEP 12

Unfold brims to make circles. Press with seams open (Figure M).

STEP 13

Pin brim circles, right sides together. Sew a seam around outer edge
(Figure N). Turn right side out, and press (Figure O).

STEP 14

Place front of brim against front of hat, with seams matching
(Figure P).

STEP 15

Pin brim all around (Figure Q). Using a zipper foot, stitch brim to hat,
about ⅛" (0.3 cm) beyond piping stitch. Zigzag raw edges.

STEP 16

Press inside seam (seam made by sewing brim to top part of hat)
upwards. Make a stitch on right side of hat, to secure inside seam
against inside of hat. This allows hat to sit comfortably on the head
(Figure R).

STEP 17

Steam hat into shape.

STEP 18

If you like, sew an 8" (20.3 cm) piece of ribbon onto each side of the
hat, for tying it onto baby's head.

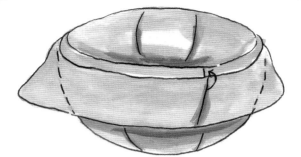

Figure P

Figure Q

Figure R

Nursing Cover for Mom

Nursing covers are a wonderful accessory for women who want to be discreet while breastfeeding their babies. This cover is simply draped over one shoulder, providing a comforting screen for your baby. After the baby has finished breastfeeding, you can use the nursing cover for burping.

EXPERIENCE LEVEL

DIMENSIONS

• Burp cloth: 13" x 46" (33 cm x 116 cm)
• With cotton gathers: 16" x 46" (40.6 cm x 116 cm)

MATERIALS

• 1 cloth diaper with premade seams cut off or 28" x 28" (71.1 cm x 71.1 cm) piece of terry cloth
• 40" x 20" (101.6 cm x 50.8 cm) piece of cotton fabric
• Matching sewing thread
• 29" (73.7 cm) decorative trim

TOOLS

• Iron
• Pins
• Scissors
• Sewing machine

> If you use cloth diapers for this project, cutting off the premade seams prevents the nursing cloth from becoming too bulky around the edges.

Instructions

STEP 1

Fold cloth diaper in half (Figure A).

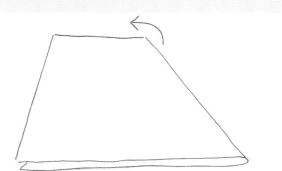

Figure A

Figure B

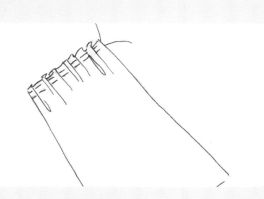

Figure C

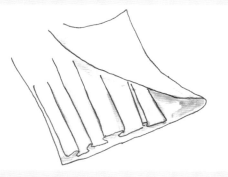

Figure D

Hem 2 long sides and 1 short side of cotton fabric (Figure B).

STEP 3

Make gathers in cotton fabric along side without hem (Figure C).

STEP 4

Sandwich cotton fabric inside folded diaper, matching gathered side of cotton fabric with one short side of folded diaper (Figure D).

STEP 5

Pin diaper and cotton fabric together, then sew a seam along sandwiched raw edge and open long side of diaper. Leave second short side of diaper open, for turning right side out (Figure E).

STEP 6

Turn diaper right side out and press. Pin decorative trim over front and back of both short ends of diaper. Sew trim at both ends of diaper, sewing along top and bottom of trim. To finish trim, fold ends under about ½" (1.3 cm), sew down, and press (Figure F).

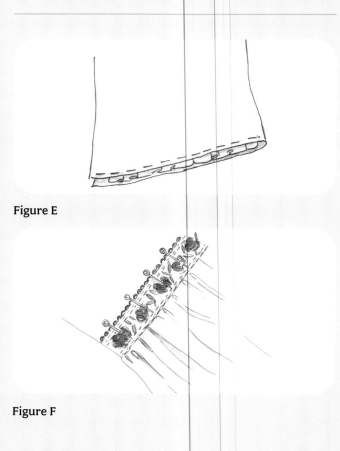

Figure E

Figure F

Trimmed Burping Cloth

Burping cloths are tiny accessories that can make a really big difference when it comes to keeping baby clean, they also help cut down on laundry! With this project, you can turn an inexpensive cloth diaper, or a piece of terry cloth or thick cotton, into a lovely burp cloth by simply adding a lovely trim.

EXPERIENCE LEVEL

DIMENSIONS

• 13½" x 27" (34 cm x 68.5 cm)

MATERIALS

• 1 cloth diaper with premade seams cut off or one 28" x 28" (71.1 cm x 71.1 cm) piece of terry cloth

• Matching sewing thread

• 60" (152.4 cm) piece of decorative trim, ruffles, or handmade bias tape

TOOLS

• Iron
• Pins
• Scissors
• Sewing machine

If you use cloth diapers, cut off the premade seams to prevent the burp cloth from becoming bulky around the edges.

Figure A

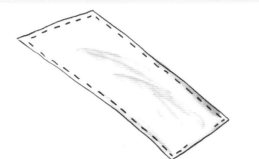

Figure B

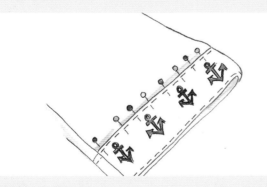

Figure C

Instructions

STEP 1

Fold diaper in half (Figure A).

STEP 2

Sew a seam all around, leaving an opening on one short side for turning right side out (Figure B).

STEP 3

Turn right side out, and slipstitch opening to close.

STEP 4

Pin decorative trim along front and back of both short edges (Figure C).

STEP 5

Sew seams along top and bottom of trim, and press.

Patterns
Farm Animal Fabric Puzzle Pattern
PHOTOCOPY PATTERNS BY 400%

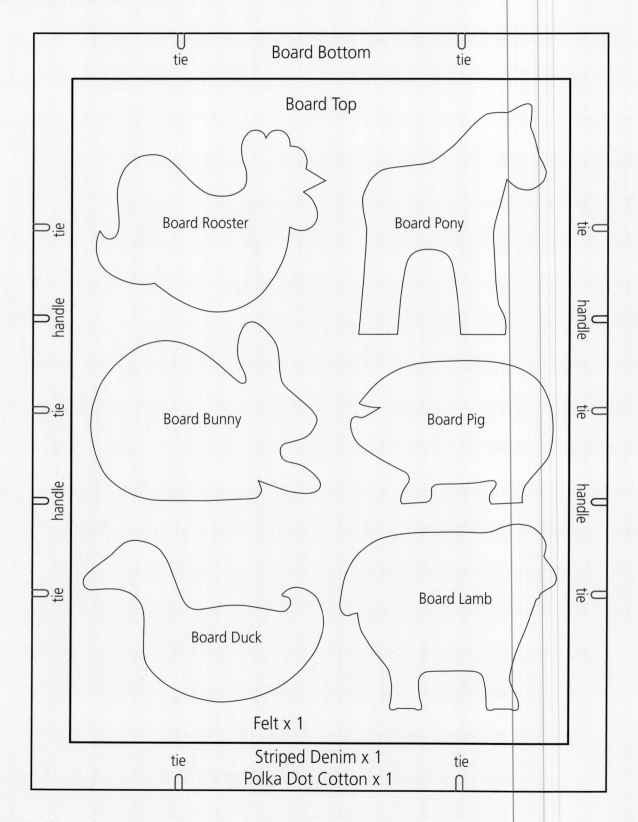

Board Bottom

tie   tie

Board Top

Board Rooster   Board Pony

tie   handle   tie   handle   tie

Board Bunny   Board Pig

Board Duck   Board Lamb

handle   tie

Felt x 1

Striped Denim x 1
Polka Dot Cotton x 1

tie   tie

Bunny

Inner Ear

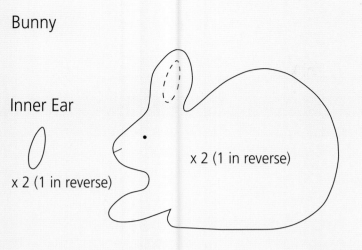

x 2 (1 in reverse)

x 2 (1 in reverse)

Sheep

Ear

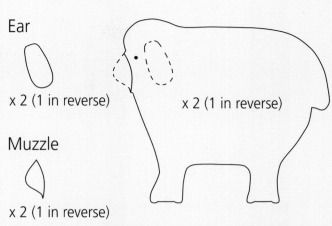

x 2 (1 in reverse)

x 2 (1 in reverse)

Muzzle

x 2 (1 in reverse)

Rooster

Beak

x 2 (1 in reverse)

Comb

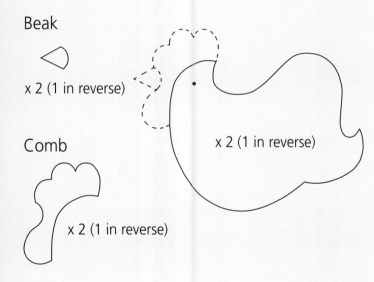

x 2 (1 in reverse)

x 2 (1 in reverse)

Pony

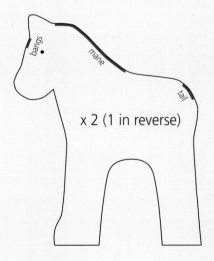

bangs

mane

tail

x 2 (1 in reverse)

Pig

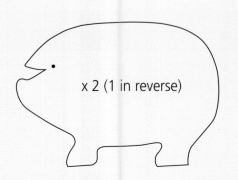

x 2 (1 in reverse)

Duck

Bill

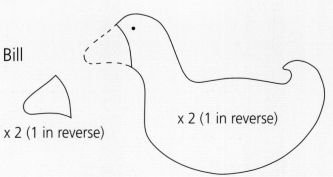

x 2 (1 in reverse)

x 2 (1 in reverse)

Mama & Baby Duck Pattern

PHOTOCOPY PATTERNS BY 200%

Baby Duck

Mama Duck

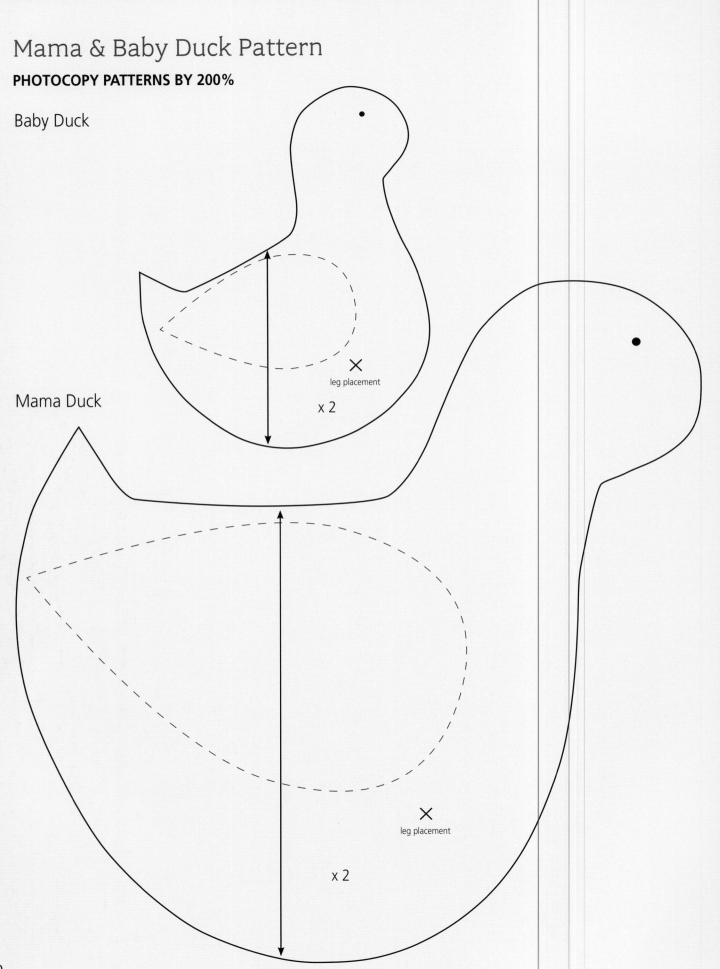

leg placement

x 2

leg placement

x 2

Baby Duck Wing

Mama Duck Wing

x 4

x 4

Baby Duck Foot

Mama Duck Foot

x 4

x 4

Baby Duck Bill

Mama Duck Bill

x 2

x 2

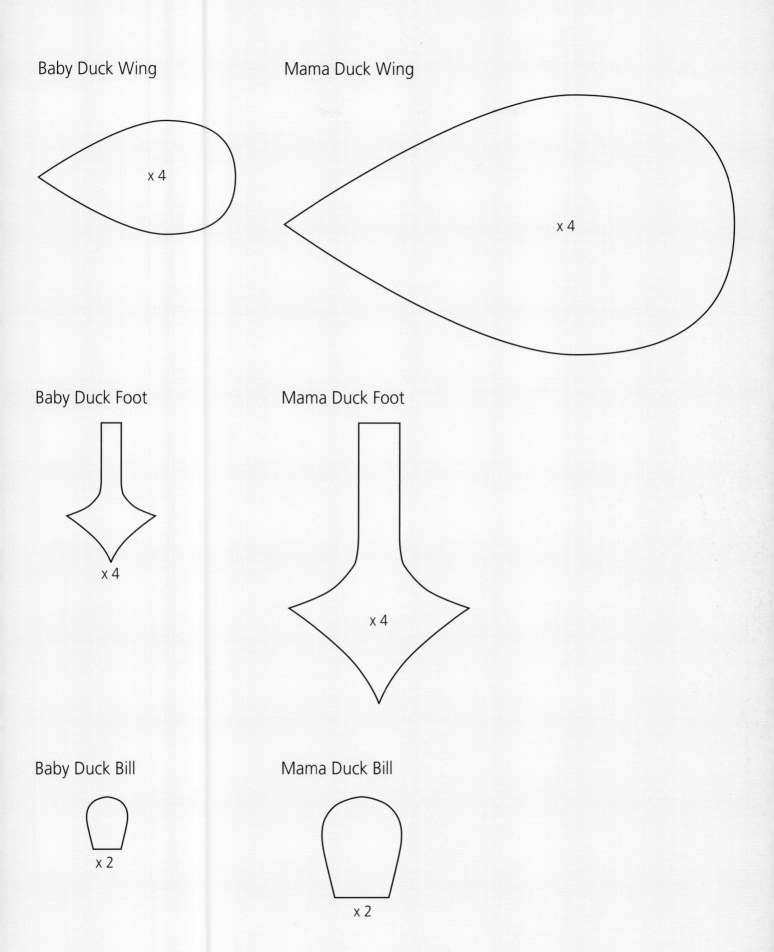

Fun and Fresh Groceries and Bag Pattern

PHOTOCOPY PATTERNS BY 200%

Bag Front/Back

Bag Handle

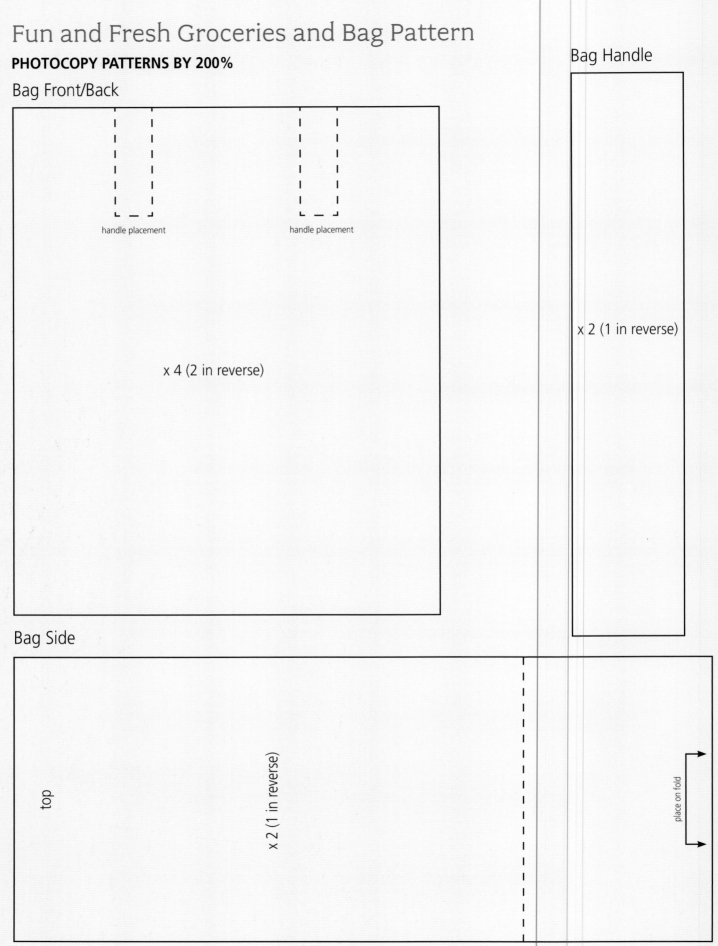

handle placement

handle placement

x 4 (2 in reverse)

x 2 (1 in reverse)

Bag Side

top

x 2 (1 in reverse)

place on fold

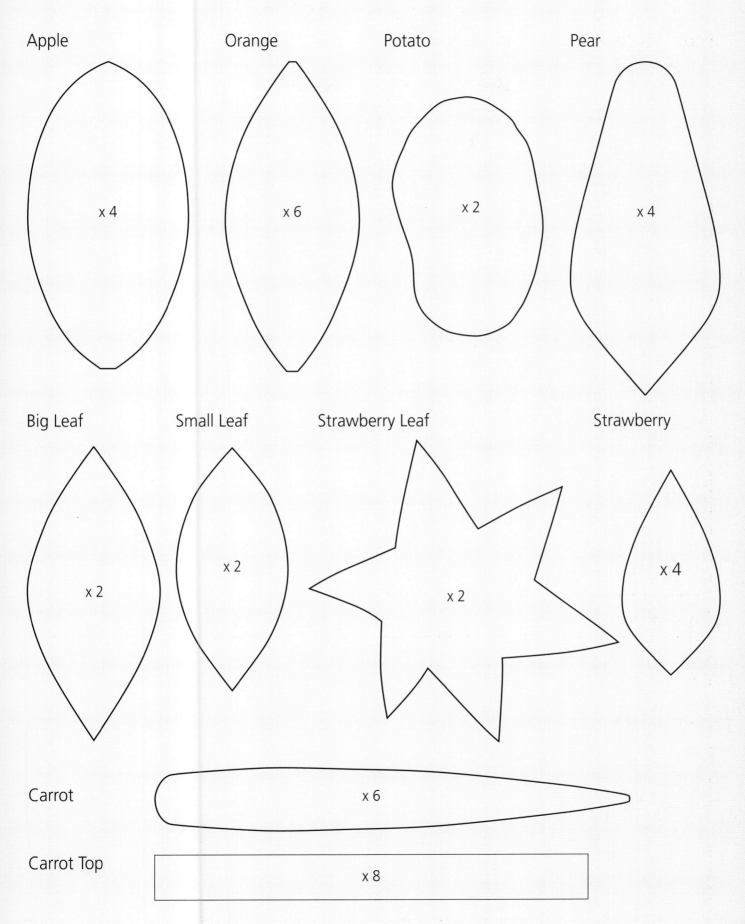

Apple x 4

Orange x 6

Potato x 2

Pear x 4

Big Leaf x 2

Small Leaf x 2

Strawberry Leaf x 2

Strawberry x 4

Carrot x 6

Carrot Top x 8

Banana Fruit

Yellow Banana Peel and White Banana Peel

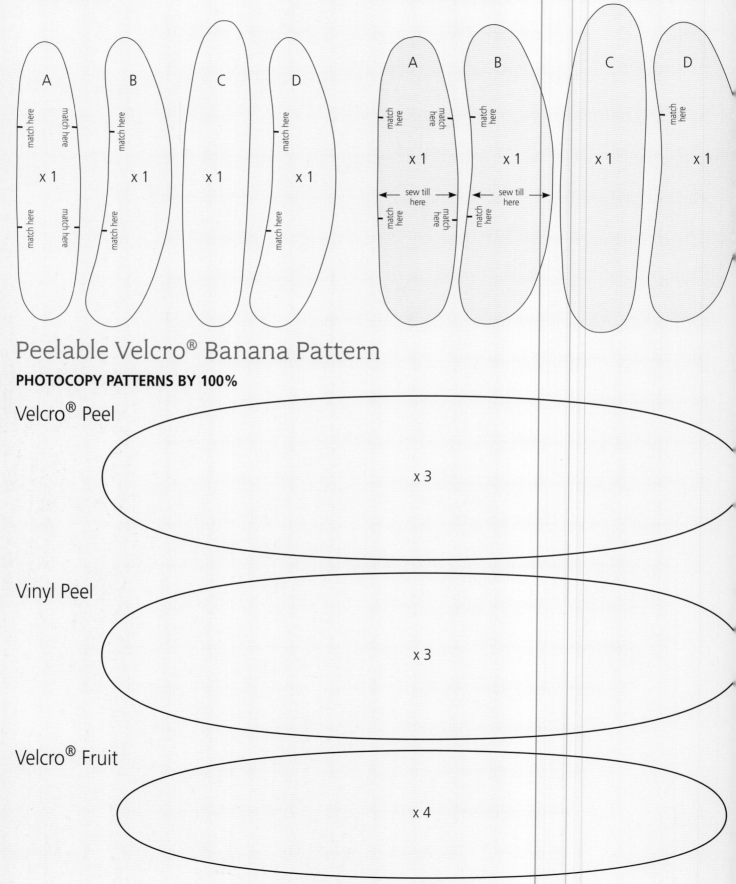

A
match here match here
x 1
match here match here

B
match here
x 1
match here

C
x 1

D
match here
x 1

A
match here match here
x 1
sew till here
match here match here

B
match here
x 1
sew till here
match here

C
x 1

D
match here
x 1

Peelable Velcro® Banana Pattern

PHOTOCOPY PATTERNS BY 100%

Velcro® Peel

x 3

Vinyl Peel

x 3

Velcro® Fruit

x 4

Crinkly Goldfish Toy Pattern

PHOTOCOPY PATTERNS BY 200%

Body

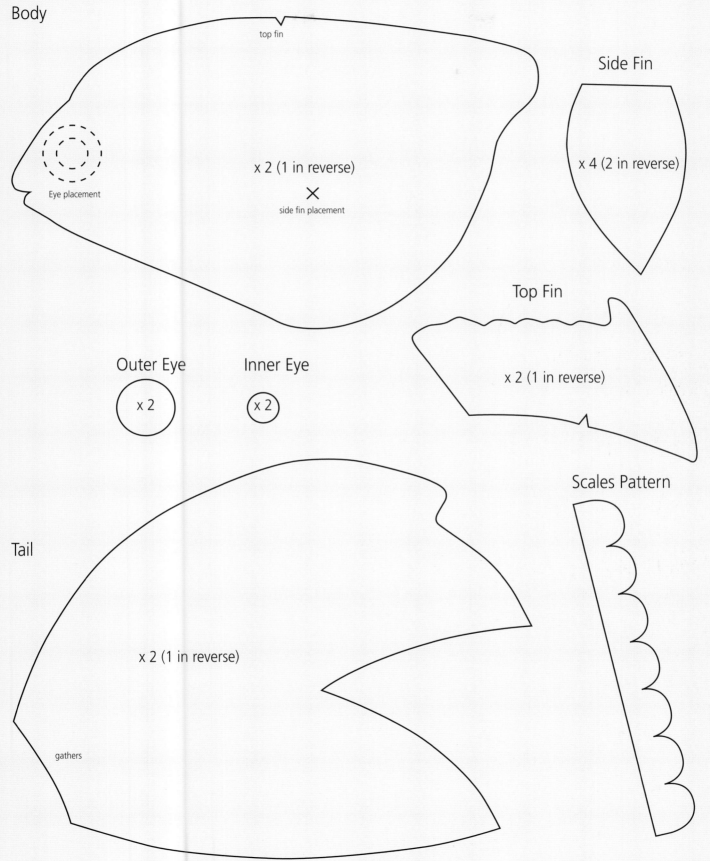

top fin

Eye placement

x 2 (1 in reverse)

✕

side fin placement

Side Fin

x 4 (2 in reverse)

Top Fin

x 2 (1 in reverse)

Outer Eye

x 2

Inner Eye

x 2

Tail

x 2 (1 in reverse)

gathers

Scales Pattern

Rattling Sheep Ball Pattern

PHOTOCOPY PATTERNS BY 100%

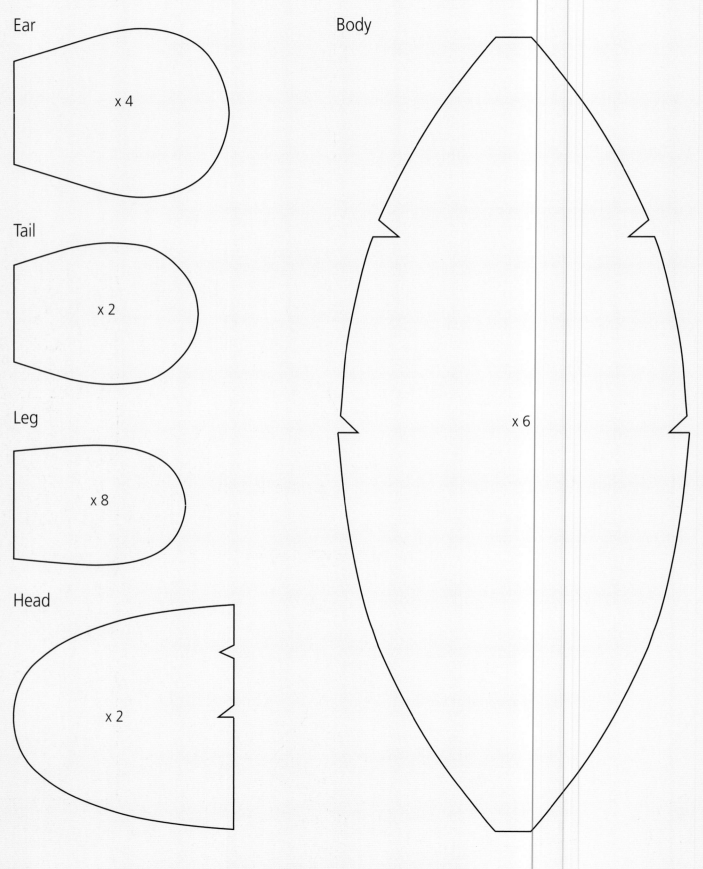

Ear

x 4

Tail

x 2

Leg

x 8

Head

x 2

Body

x 6

Soft and Funky Buildings Shapes Pattern

PHOTOCOPY PATTERNS BY 400%

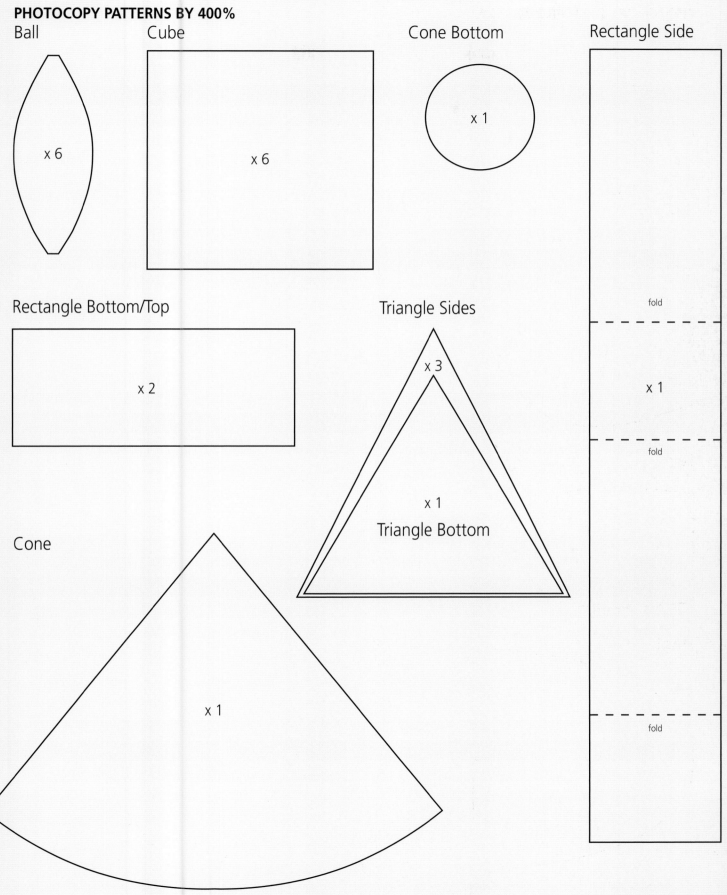

Ball

Cube

Cone Bottom

Rectangle Side

x 6

x 6

x 1

Rectangle Bottom/Top

x 2

Triangle Sides

x 3

x 1

Triangle Bottom

fold

x 1

fold

Cone

x 1

fold

Striped Scallop-Edged Blanket Pattern

PHOTOCOPY PATTERN BY 800%

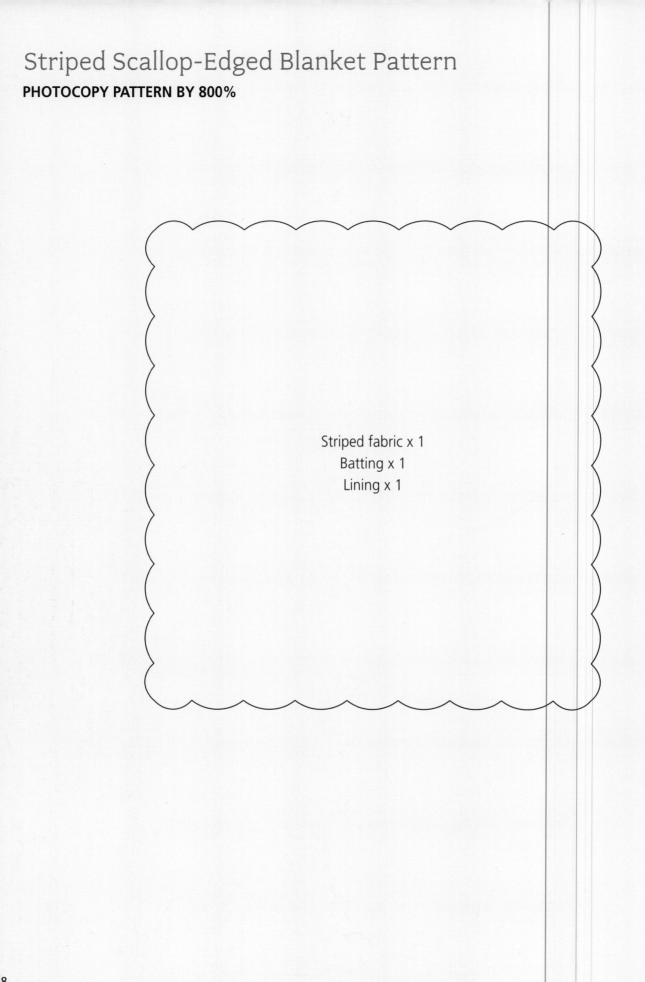

Striped fabric x 1
Batting x 1
Lining x 1

Baby's First Book Pattern

PHOTOCOPY PATTERNS BY 300%

Foam

x 6

Inside Page

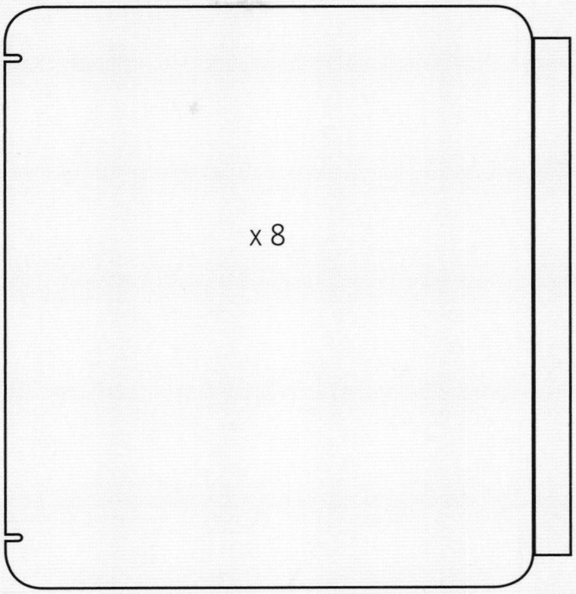

x 8

Last Page

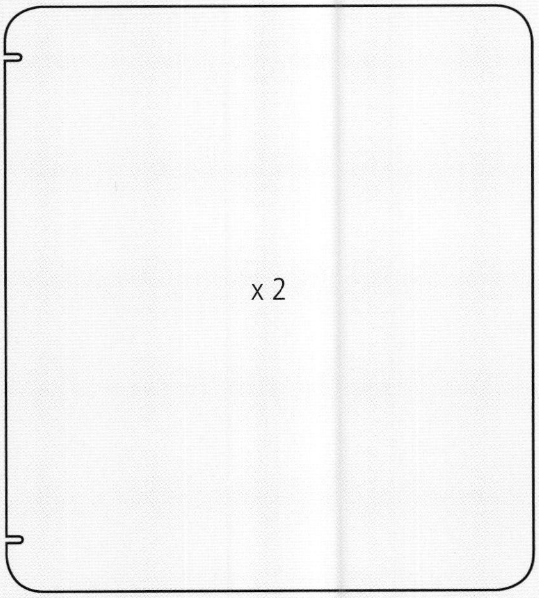

x 2

Cover

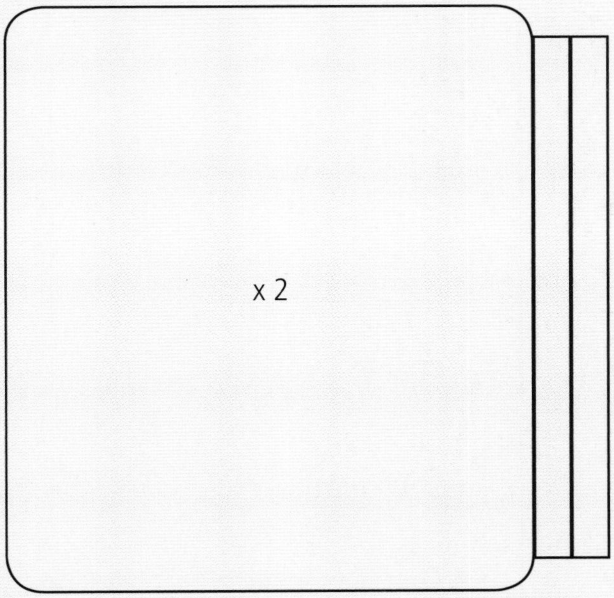

x 2

Shapes for Appliqué

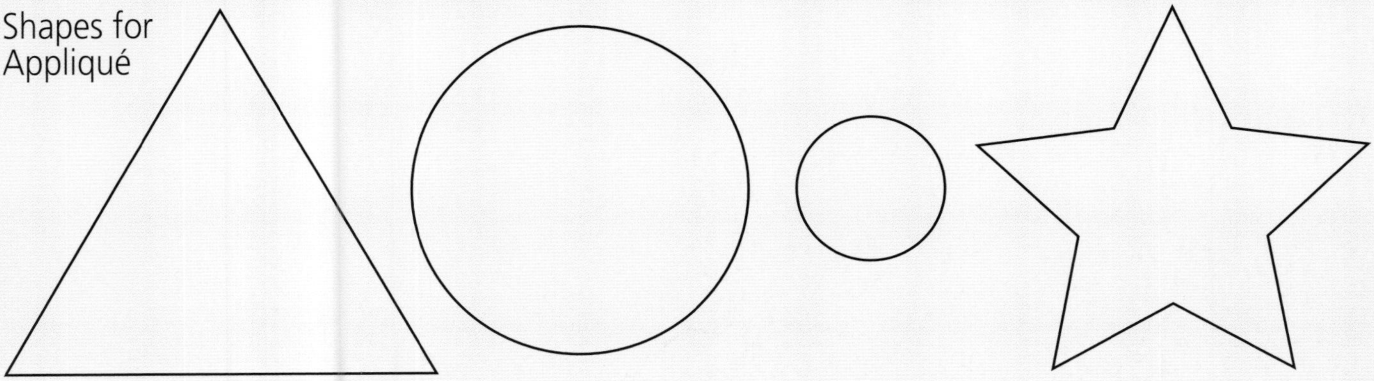

Awake/Asleep Elephant Sachet Pattern

PHOTOCOPY PATTERNS BY 125%

Elephant

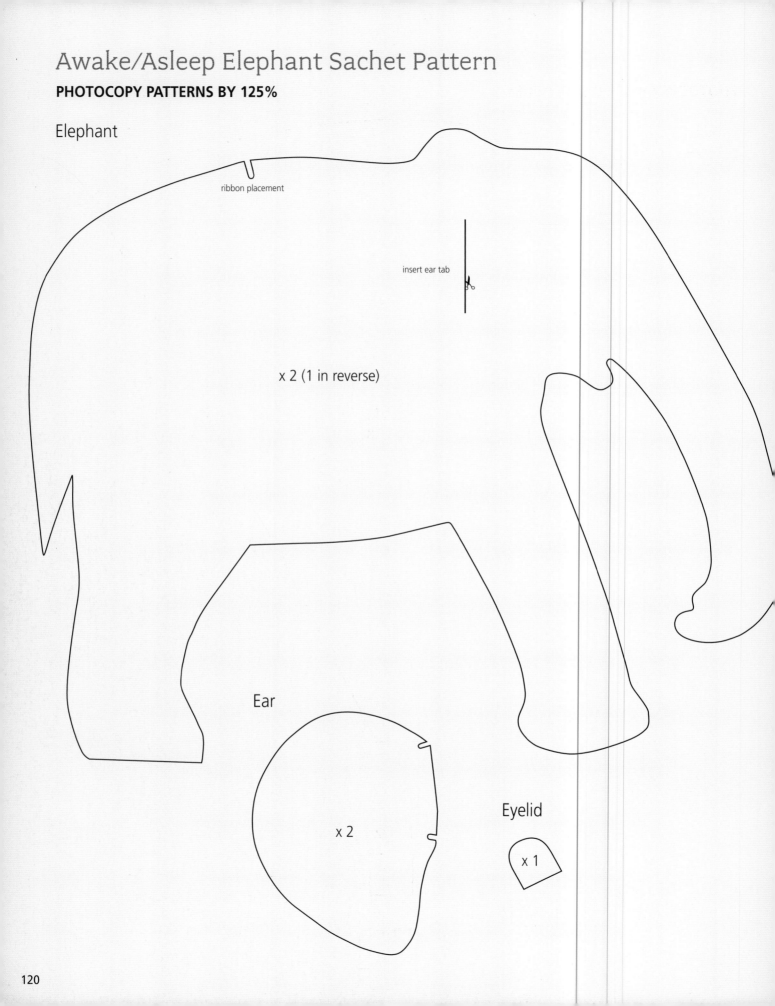

ribbon placement

insert ear tab

x 2 (1 in reverse)

Ear

x 2

Eyelid

x 1

Count-the-Sheep-to-Sleep Mobile Pattern

PHOTOCOPY PATTERNS BY 120%

Mobile

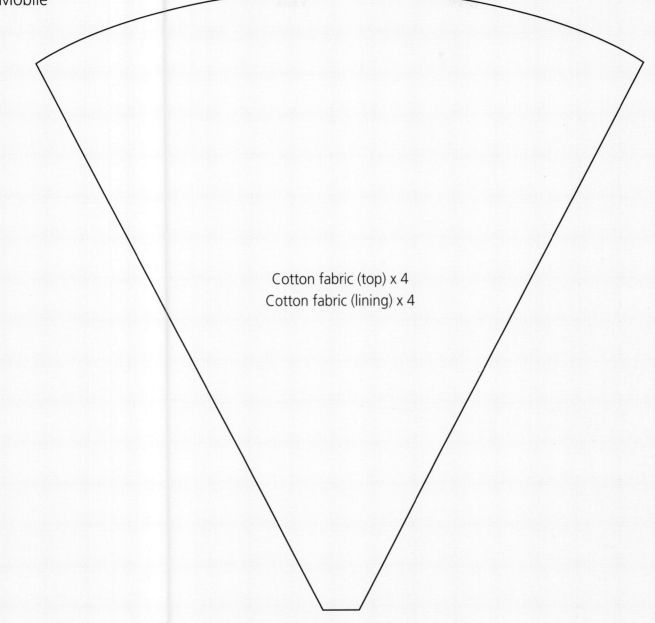

Cotton fabric (top) x 4
Cotton fabric (lining) x 4

Parts for four Sheep

Ear

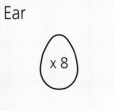

x 8

Leg

x 16

Muzzle

x 4

Bird-in-Nest Pattern
PHOTOCOPY PATTERNS BY 125%

Bird

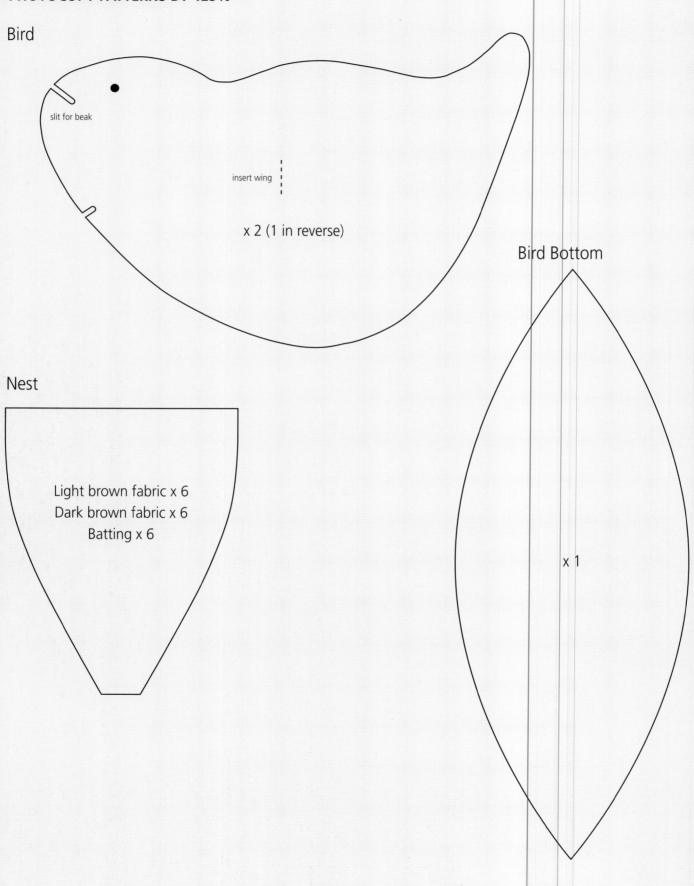

slit for beak

insert wing

x 2 (1 in reverse)

Bird Bottom

Nest

Light brown fabric x 6
Dark brown fabric x 6
Batting x 6

x 1

Family Photo Cube Pattern

PHOTOCOPY PATTERNS BY 200%

Photo Cube

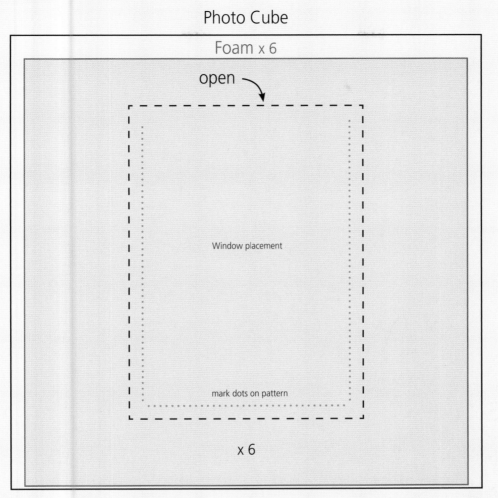

Foam x 6

open

Window placement

mark dots on pattern

x 6

Window

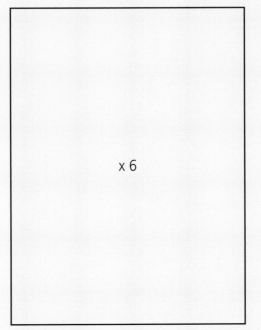

x 6

Bunny-Carrot-Bunny Flag Pattern
PHOTOCOPY PATTERNS BY 120%

Bunny

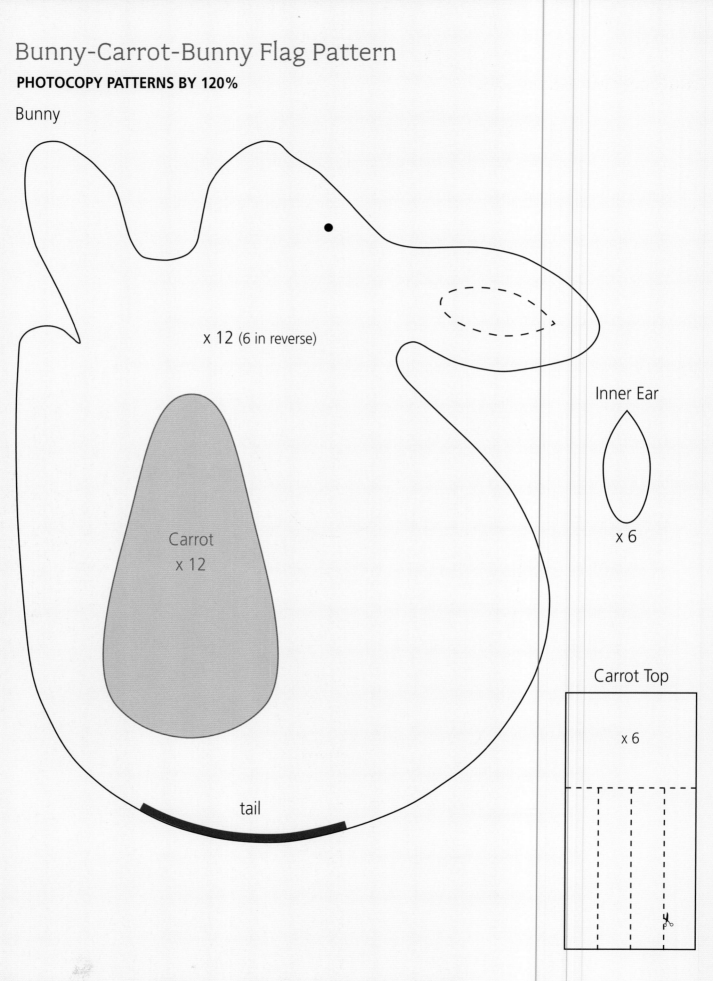

x 12 (6 in reverse)

Carrot
x 12

tail

Inner Ear

x 6

Carrot Top

x 6

Baby Bear Bib Pattern

PHOTOCOPY PATTERNS BY 400%

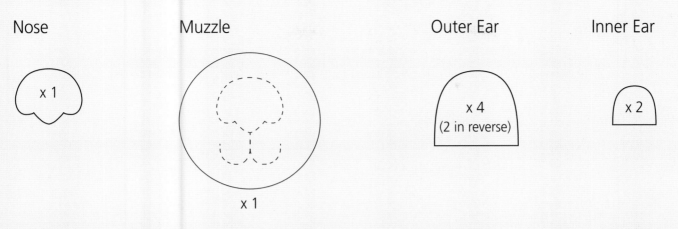

Nose

x 1

Muzzle

x 1

Outer Ear

x 4
(2 in reverse)

Inner Ear

x 2

Bib

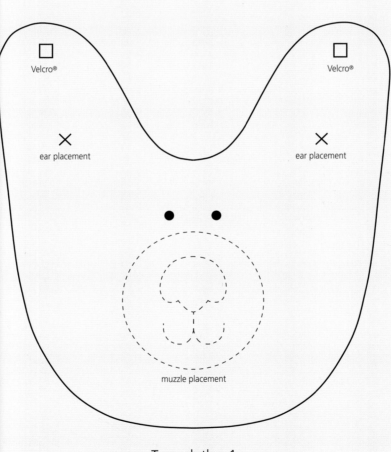

Velcro®

Velcro®

✕
ear placement

✕
ear placement

muzzle placement

Terry cloth x 1
Lining x 1

Striped Baby Bib Pattern

PHOTOCOPY PATTERN BY 125%

Bib

Cotton back x 1
Striped fabric x 1

Adorable Elf Slippers Pattern

PHOTOCOPY PATTERNS BY 125%

Sole

Lining

Cotton x 2
Foam x 2
Vinyl x 2

x 4 (2 in reverse)

Slipper

x 4 (2 in reverse)

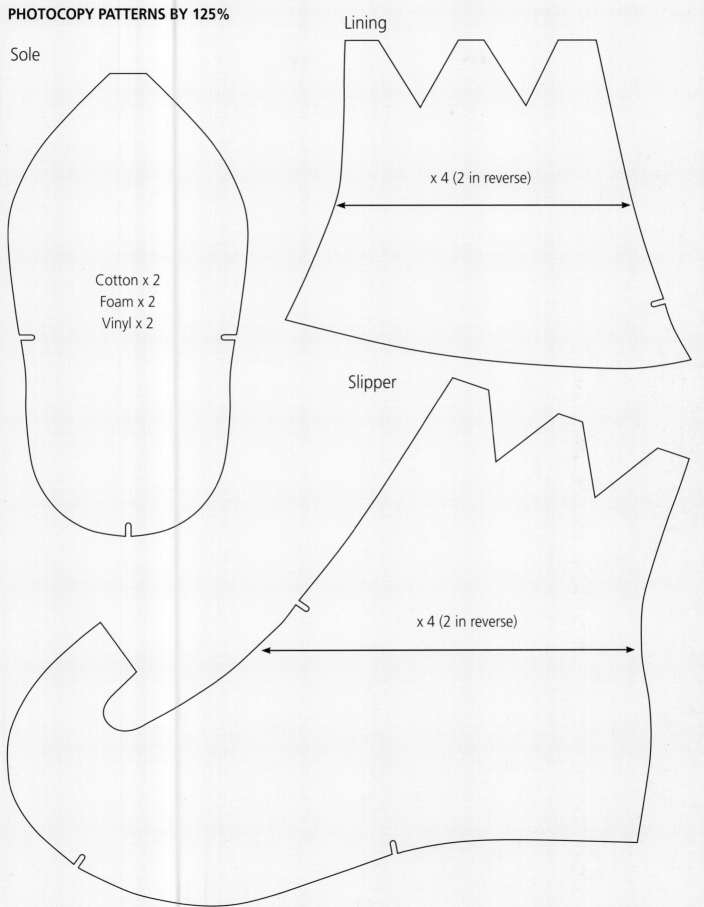

Puppy Sunhat Pattern

PHOTOCOPY PATTERNS BY 200%

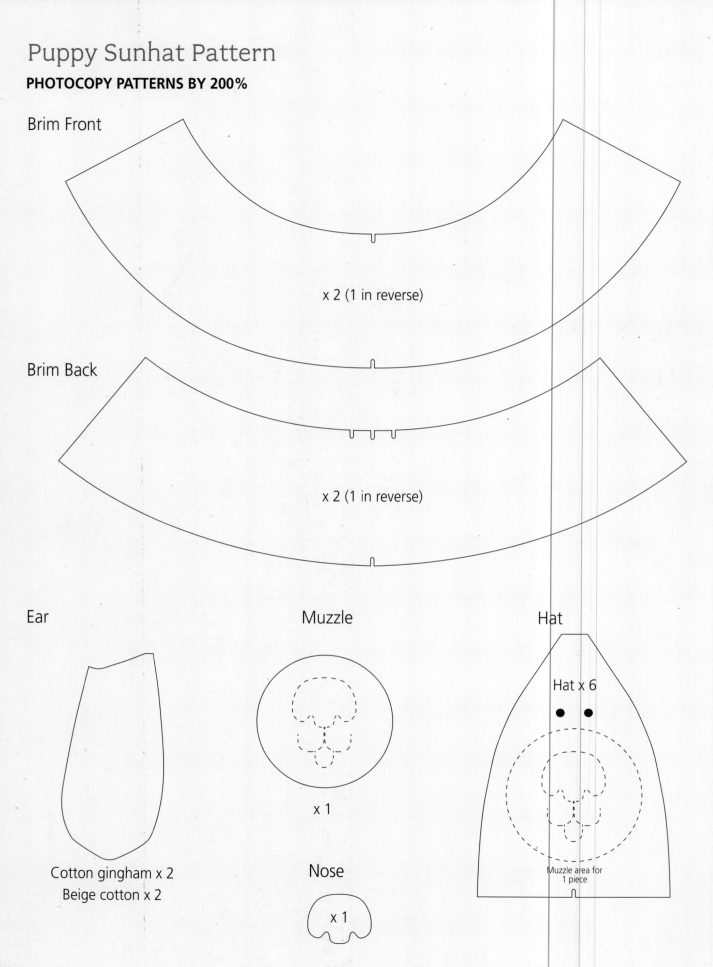

Brim Front

x 2 (1 in reverse)

Brim Back

x 2 (1 in reverse)

Ear

Cotton gingham x 2
Beige cotton x 2

Muzzle

x 1

Nose

x 1

Hat

Hat x 6

Muzzle area for
1 piece